FISHING
NEW
ZEALAND

Copyright © Adam Clancey, 2005
Copyright © David Bateman Ltd, 2005

Published 2005 by David Bateman Ltd,
30 Tarndale Grove, Albany, Auckland, New Zealand

ISBN 1-86953-585-5

Photo credits: page 45, Ninety Mile Beach, Destination Northland; pages 55, 75, 93, 100 and
155, Russell McGeorge.

Designed by Red Design, Auckland
Printed in China through Everbest Printing Company Ltd

FISHING
NEW
ZEALAND

Adam Clancey

David Bateman

Contents

Preface

My first defining moment in fishing happened some years ago as a young child in England. My parents would send me off fishing when we were away camping. My 'hot spot' was a picturesque river directly in front of the family caravan. The quarry was an array of minnows with names like gudgeon, bleak and red throats, none of which grew bigger than a few inches long.

On one occasion, one of my captures was foul-hooked, and being unable to remove the hook, I thought I would let the fish swim around under the float until an adult could assist me with its release. After a few minutes my rod took on a bend like never before and I landed what was at that time the largest fish I had ever caught – a redfin perch of about half a pound.

This magnificent fish was the talk of the camp and, unbeknown to me, was the start of what has turned out to be an all-consuming passion, career and lifestyle. On that particular day, that possie was the best fishing spot in the world!

For the next defining moment, fast-forward a few years and halfway round the globe to New Zealand, where I was fishing off some rocks on the Auckland waterfront. Sprats and piper were my quarry and my skills, tackle and knowledge had all improved.

Every carefully baited hook would attract a strike from an unsuspecting baitfish. While staring into a mass of baitfish, I noticed some odd behaviour: all the little fish suddenly began swimming in one direction. Then, out of nowhere, three huge fish, the likes of which I had never encountered before, smashed right through them. I had to catch one of these spectacular looking fish! So started my quest to catch a yellowtail kingfish, which has since expanded to a total love of sportfishing and an interest in fish generally.

My brother Matthew and I rigging up to fish on a salmon river in Scotland.
Photo: Doug Clancey.

To make the most of the information provided within these pages, it is important to understand the style of fishing and the techniques I employ, usually successfully. If you are looking for a 'cure-all' for your fishing, read carefully, as the keys to consistently catching fish are all here. The rule I apply to my fishing is: Expect to catch your best fish every time you go fishing, but don't be disappointed if you succeed in just having a good day out.

If you are the kind of fisherman who finds a good spot and rapes it until it is barren, perhaps you should consider this: the joy you experience in taking a child back to a spot 20 years after you found it, teaching him or her the secrets of how to fish it and sharing your knowledge, experience and love of fishing will greatly outweigh the short-term gratification of catching heaps of fish.

Some of the spots mentioned in this book are very location-specific; others, due to their vast area, are general guides for success when fishing in that region. I have not included GPS co-ordinates for any of the spots in this book. While a GPS is a valuable navigation tool, able to guide you to and from a specific area, it won't guarantee fishing success. For consistent success, it's just as important to take into account all the environmental factors at any fishing possie, because the tide or wind can affect a spot considerably.

I dedicate this book to all the anglers who have ever shared their knowledge with me – whether it was knots, baits, rigs or fishing spots. With this book I am able to share a part of what I have learned, gleaned or some way extracted from your experiences and my own – it is as much yours as it is mine.

Adam Clancey
2005

Fishing is a gift that should be passed on through the generations. Raven Clancey-Peetz is definitely following in his Dad's footsteps.

Introduction

Do the basics well

This book is a guide, and while it makes specific reference to some spots, others are dealt with in more general terms. It is unlikely fish will be in exactly the same spot every time you go fishing, and making a spot fire involves far more than just going there to fish. In this introduction the key elements for success will be discussed. Missing out one important element can make the difference between success and failure, so I have tried to deliver all the elements for each spot with special emphasis on the most critical. Do read the information in this introduction, as it is a basis for the way I approach all my fishing... and remember, when it comes to fishing, you never stop learning.

Getting it right can be as simple as a well-tied knot.

Tackle

Tackle choice will influence success more than you can imagine; something as simple as selecting a hook does makes a difference. The following overview points out some fundamentals of fishing tackle, and as you read through the spots, I will make specific reference to what tackle to use and any other equipment that is useful.

The sea is the harshest environment in the world. Fishing tackle needs maintenance to perform properly. You wouldn't expect your car to go if you filled the engine up with sand and salt.

Rods and reels: Whatever fishing outfits you decide to use, stick with the best quality you can afford. The possibly thousands of options are best dealt with by visiting a professional tackle store. They should ask you a lot of questions about your fishing before they narrow down a range to show you. An experienced tackle expert will mix and match options and show you outfits that are balanced in the hand and suit many techniques.

The worst mistake is to begin by looking at price tags when you start shopping. Go in with an open mind. Search the Internet and consult other anglers. If you only have a limited budget, buy the best you can get for your money.

While it is important to have good tackle, it is far more important that the tackle you use is well maintained. More good fish are lost due to poorly maintained equipment than to any other cause. The key points are: reels should be full of fresh line of the correct breaking strain; the drag must be fully functional – smooth and progressive in its settings, not jerky, shuddering or going from freespool to lockup in half a turn; moving parts, such as bail arms and handles, should be working and properly lubricated. Finally, any broken parts should be replaced.

Rods should have a complete set of rings with no grooves in the eyes and the winch fitting should secure the reel without any play.

Always keep reels full of line.

Line: Fishing line is possibly the most misunderstood piece of equipment and the part most commonly blamed for lost fish. I can honestly say I have never lost a fish due to line failure. Sure, I have broken off more times than I care to remember, but the reasons vary from applying too much pressure (angler error) to damage in the line caused by tangles or crossed lines (angler error).

There is no such thing as bad fishing line. There is, however, a world of difference in the properties of monofilament.

For example, take your average mini-bulk spool of 15 kg monofilament. This line may break anywhere from, say, 13 kg to 17 kg on the same spool, so you have to allow for this when setting your drag. The normal procedure is to set your drag at one-third of your line's breaking strain, i.e., 15 kg = 5 kg, leaving you with 10 kg in reserve. But poor knot-tying may further reduce the breaking strain to 50%, and remember parts of your line are only 13 kg to begin with (50% of 13 kg is just 6.5 kg).

Now, let's say you hook a good fish and you have 100 m of line in the water. The water pressure would add another 1 kg (6.5 kg – 1 kg = 5.5 kg). The fish is running out line easily so you add a little more pressure with your thumb, maybe 3 kg (5.5 kg – 3 kg = 2.5 kg). All of a sudden your line breaks. And you were using 15 kg line!

Cheaper lines generally have a lot of memory, are fairly thick in diameter and break down reasonably quickly when exposed to the sun's ultraviolet (UV) rays. Cheap line may be fine for pulling in a bunch of schoolie snapper in the Rangitoto Channel, and provided it is changed regularly – about once a year – it will perform OK. Put the same line to the test on a 25 kg kingfish and it may not fare so well.

At the other end of the scale, take a high-quality monofilament line. This line will have uniform breaking strain – 15 kg will break at 1 kg either side of its claimed breaking strain – and it will usually feature polymers that keep the line soft and pliable, making it easier to tie good knots. Good quality lines also have fairly uniform stretch characteristics. Stretch acts as a cushion, absorbing shock from sudden runs or jarring strikes. Good lines are made with various properties to suit different environments. Some are very thin, which allows less wind resistance for better casting. Others have tough exteriors to protect against abrasion.

Terminal tackle: Terminal tackle describes the bits you put on the end of your line and includes hooks, sinkers, trace, swivels and sinkers.

Sinkers: are fairly easy to deal with, as they have two basic functions: either

It pays to carry a good selection of terminal tackle.

to get your line to the bottom, or to give you distance when casting.

Although sinkers come in hundreds of different shapes and sizes, they can be broken down to two categories: ones the line passes through (running sinkers) and ones that the line ties to (fixed sinkers).

Using the right amount of weight is critical. Most rods designed for casting have a cast weight recommendation (cast weight). Stick to this and the rod will respond by casting well.

There is no real rule of thumb to selecting a sinker to use for getting your bait to the bottom – there are too many variables. When straylining you want your bait to sink slowly to the bottom without getting snagged, so you need just enough weight to carry the bait down with the current to the bottom. You may have to change your sinker size several times to compensate for changes in tidal flow or wind effects as the fishing day progresses.

Have a variety of sinkers.

When fishing a dropper rig over a reef for tarakihi or blue cod, you want it to go straight down, quickly. So a hydrodynamically shaped sinker that overcomes any current is ideal.

Sinker selection can make the difference between catching a feed and drawing a blank when drift-fishing. Too much weight and your bait hangs very uninvitingly and snags up too often; too little weight and your bait lifts out of the strike zone. A correctly weighted sinker allows you to keep your bait moving, covering the ground while staying in contact with the bottom.

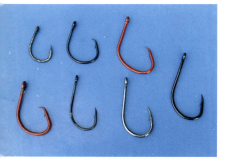

Hooks: come in all shapes and sizes and they all catch fish. But hook selection can play a large part in success or failure. Again, physics plays a big part, as does common sense. For example, say you are using a 6 kg outfit in 20 m of water. You're straylining for snapper with a heavy-gauge, blunt, 8/0 hook tied to the end of your line. Now the amount of pressure required to set that hook through a fish's bony jaw may be 3 kg plus. And the stretch in the line may be 15%, so your chances of consistently setting the hook are greatly reduced compared to, say, a 6/0, fine-gauge, chemically-sharpened hook.

Imagine another scenario: a 1/0, fine-wire hook, fished in 100 m of water with 24 kg superbraid line. Chances are any decent-sized fish will straighten or break the hook.

Hooks, even hooks of the same size, have different wire gauges, strengths and applications. Three styles – suicide, circle and livebait – would suit most conditions you are likely to encounter. Match them to the size of bait and the tackle rather than the size of fish you are trying to catch. You do not need every size. Go for evens, i.e., 2/0, 4/0, 6/0, 8/0 and 10/0.

The different finishes are a matter of taste. Some people prefer red for camouflaging in the bait and some anglers like nickel-plated hooks for superior rust resistance. Most important of all, whichever hook you choose, make sure it is sharp!

Trace: is the part of the rig that is normally made up of monofilament, and in some cases, wire. The whole idea of a trace is to give extra protection at the business end of your line. Teeth, sharp gill plates, rocks and scuffs can weaken your main line to breaking point, whereas a heavier trace offers extra protection.

A lot of anglers fish with a trace lighter than their main line to save sinkers if they get snagged. Now this, to my mind, is totally wrong. I'd rather lose a few sinkers and land a fish of a lifetime.

Determining the right length of trace is down to you. In most cases a rod-length is ample, with the exception of big game fishing and extreme situations.

While a heavy trace offers protection from abrasion, using too thick a trace may scare shy-feeding fish and will not present as well as finer trace. It's a trade-off – lighter trace, more bites and more bust-offs; heavier trace, fewer bust-offs but fewer bites as well.

I always carry at least three different weights and mix and match to suit the conditions.

Lures: Fishing with lures is very rewarding and productive. A small selection of lures in your tackle box will give you the advantage of being able to employ a raft of other fishing techniques, such as jigging, trolling and spinning. Understanding how each technique is used and when to use it will dictate what lures you keep in your box.

You could fill the pages of a hundred books trying to explain the finer points of lure fishing, and many fishermen with great experience have already published excellent volumes on the subject. The following little story puts it into context.

A fisherman began fishing alongside a group of us at a river mouth where kahawai were chasing whitebait. My friends and I were hooking up more or less every cast using small, fish-shaped lures about the size of the whitebait, 3 m casting rods and 6 kg line. This guy set up his boat rod with an old eggbeater reel spooled with about 50 m of 20 kg line. First he tried bait with no success. Then we suggested he try a lure if he had one. From his kit he produced an old white plastic lure with a very large double-hook. This lure is well known as a trolling lure, but it has no integral weight – the thing was nearly useless with his tackle, and anyway, his retrieve action was far too slow. He could only cast it 10 m at best.

I felt a bit sorry for this guy, as you could see he was obviously very keen to get into the action. So I took a spool of 10 kg line and refilled his reel for him and rigged him up with a casting lure. On about his third cast he hooked up and landed a big fat kahawai, followed by a couple more in quick succession.

When he left he said that was the first time he had caught a fish on a lure. I explained that the lure he had was perfect if he were trolling from a boat among a school of kahawai, but it was not a casting lure.

The point of this story is quite simple. There is no one lure that fits every scenario, so a selection suited to the different styles and techniques is a must.

I would categorise lures in four general groups.

This lure obviously looked real.

Trolling lures: are designed to be dragged behind a boat. The motion of being towed imparts an action to the lure, which attracts predators. The best time to troll is when you can see obvious signs of fish predators or prey on the surface, or if you are prospecting a new piece of territory.

Trolling lures can vary in size from a 3 cm silver spoon to a massive resin-head marlin lure over half a metre long. Choosing the right size is dictated by the size of baitfish the predators are eating.

Jigging/casting: A jig is a weighted lure that is often shaped like fish. A jig is designed to be cast or dropped to the bottom and either yo-yoed up and down close to the bottom, or retrieved quickly from the bottom. Most jigs also make good casting lures.

Trolling lures come in a huge range of shapes and sizes.

Try to 'match the hatch' by using a lure that most resembles the size of the baitfish.

Carry a variety of jigs to suit the depth and current.

I suggest that you choose lures that are sturdy in construction. Light hooks and split rings will fail at the most inopportune times. Jigs are generally most effective when drift-fishing among fish schooling in mid-water or near the bottom.

Poppers/surface lures: create a lot of disturbance and attract spectacular strikes from predators. They work by imitating a baitfish trying to escape across the surface.

Poppers and surface lures are most effective when cast and retrieved with an erratic action the angler imparts using the rod. The ideal areas to use them are structures where predators hunt. These may be channel markers or reefs with lots of white water. They're also useful when larger predators are actively surface-feeding on larger baitfish such as piper or mullet.

Sabikis and flashers: consist of multiple flies tied on a dropper rig. The hooks vary in size from #14, for catching sprats and piper, to 10/0 for hapuku.

Flashers and sabikis are effective used without bait, but their performance can be enhanced by adding a small strip of bait. Baited flashers/sabikis are deadly on all species.

The most common way of using flashers is to tie a fixed sinker at the bottom of the rig and lower to just off the bottom. Flasher rigs are ideal when drift-fishing, as the rocking motion of the boat adds action to the lures. Flashers are equally effective when fished in the surf, as the wave action works the rig.

'Sabiki' is the Japanese name given to the smaller version of flashers. They are primarily used for catching baitfish. Use them in exactly the same way as flashers and you will nearly always have a way of catching livebaits.

Kids can have hours of fun on any wharf in the country with a small spinning rod rigged with sabikis – and they'll catch bait for your next fishing trip!

Fished in the right way, flashers and sabikis are deadly.

Bait

Whether you catch your own, or buy it from tackle store, bait should always be in good condition. A bag of pilchards that has been refrozen three times is only good for berley. I like to use a variety of different baits. They may consist of pilchards, squid, skipjack (bonito) or freshly caught piper and yellowtail.

There are times when fish prefer one bait over another and certain species prefer certain bait. For example, some fish only eat crustaceans and shellfish, so fishing with pilchards and bonito would be pointless. If I was targeting kingfish, a freshly caught piper is the next best thing to livebait, whereas a fresh sprat, even a live one, may be totally ignored.

Another useful tip for choosing bait: If you are trying to avoid small fish picking at soft baits, change to a hard bait such as a fresh strip of kahawai able to stand the attention of the pickers until a reasonable specimen comes along.

Big baits definitely attract big fish. If you are targeting big snapper, large baits such as half a mullet or a bonito head will turn up trumps if there are any moochers in the area. You will get fewer bites, but the bites you do get will be worthwhile.

The use of novelty baits, such as liver soaked in kerosene, has foundation and one should never stop experimenting with baits.

Berley comes in just about any recipe you can think of.

Berley: Ground bait, berley, chum – it's all the same. Berley can be as simple as a piece of bread used to attract sprats at a wharf, or concoctions with tuna oil, cooked rice, sand and mussel. Berley serves two main purposes: firstly it attracts small fish to feed, that in turn attract larger predators. Secondly, the scent of food in the water will draw fish from near and far and stimulate them to feed.

How effective is berley? If you went to the same spot every day and threw in two buckets of good berley, I guarantee in a very short space of time that spot would be teeming with fish. Berley attracts fish!

If there are few fish where you are fishing, you need to bring them to you with berley.

Conditions

When a set of conditions come together a spot may fire up. The majority of conditions are climatic and seasonal. Others can be associated with the availability of food. For example, when the water temperature in the Hauraki Gulf reaches 16.9ºC, snapper colour up, move into groups, and start their pre-spawning activity. These fish can be found schooling in large numbers over the sand in the outer Hauraki Gulf before running into the harbours through the Rangitoto and Motuihe Channels, where they are easy prey for anglers.

Another good example is when a particularly high tide coincides with a storm, dislodging lots of food like shellfish and smashed kina. The fish move close into the shore to feed after the storm.

Don't just look at one condition, i.e., the tide's right. Try to match a set of conditions, such as, the tide is incoming at first light, the weather is overcast, wind and tide are in the same direction and the water is still discoloured after a recent storm.

Tides: You need to consider the state of tide, incoming or outgoing, the tidal range, which means how far the tide will come in and go out, and the flow – its direction and speed, called tidal stream.

Fish move around with the tides. Having a good understanding of where fish will be during any part of the tide will help your catch rate and give you more options of where to fish. Some spots will fire only on a rising tide and vice versa, because the current will hit a structure or reef, causing fish-attracting currents.

Areas of very high current and tidal flow may only be fished over slack water. Some of the spots around the Marlborough Sounds where the outgoing tide creates whirlpools and huge pressure waves are too difficult or dangerous to fish except at slack tide.

Some days you should just stay home.

Strong currents can create alleys where bait and food are pushed into a concentrated area, which attracts larger fish looking for an easy feed.

Tidal range is especially important when fishing inshore and from surf beaches, because a hole that is out of casting range on an average tide may be in range on a very low tide. Or an extra metre of water in shallow areas may offer spots that are normally too shallow to consider fishing.

Keeping a diary of trips will build up a picture of when the tides and conditions are favourable.

Local knowledge is very useful when fishing spots that you are not familiar with. Don't be afraid to ask the locals, but ask the right questions: tide, time, bait, species and time of year.

Other days are made for fishing.

The reason you really have to pick the brains of local anglers is that, while they may happily give up a spot where they have fond memories of catching lots of big fish – they may even tell you which tide and conditions to fish it – they may also neglect to tell you that this particular spot only fires in the middle of winter, so you'd be wasting your time there for three-quarters of the year.

Moon phase: One of the great mysteries of fishing is whether or not the moon affects fishing success. We all know that the gravitational effects of the moon influence the tides, and many cultures use solunar tables to judge when the fishing will be best. This is a question I can't answer and would not like to theorise about. I accept that the moon plays a big part in how fish feed – some species feed better on a waning moon and others are more active on a full moon – but I don't read more into it than that.

The best fable about fishing the moon was told to me by an old Maori chap. His reasoning was that when the moon was bad, instead of catching a canoe-full of fish, you might only get half a canoe, and that was still better than the guy who caught diddly-squat because he wasn't a skilful fisherman.

Current: Tidal, oceanic or caused by rivers, currents are good for fishing. Currents create the corridors travelled by all life in the sea. Sometimes current will work to your advantage, other times against you. Any spot where current hits structure is the first place to start looking for fish. Rocky headlands, sandbars, underwater reefs and islands – when you think about it, all good fishing spots have an area of noticeable current nearby.

Where current hits structure you can expect to find a fishing hot spot.

The main factors when fishing in a current are:

• Make sure the wind and current are travelling in the same direction or the strength of the current has a greater effect than the wind.

• Work out where the fish are likely to be sitting in the current, as it is not normally where the strongest part of the flow is.

• When you are using berley, decide where your berley will end up and draw fish from.

Temperature: Don't look for polar bears in Hawaii! Most species of fish have a water temperature range that they are most comfortable in. For some species this means following warm water currents around the globe, for others it may cause them to move to deeper water as inshore water warms up.

Water temperature is the main reason that the predominant species in the North Island and South Island differ. Also, water temperature controls, to a lesser degree, growth rates.

The blue cod is a good example. Blue cod are caught throughout New Zealand, but areas that have consistently cool water have more and bigger blue cod. Yellowtail kingfish, on the other hand, are present in the upper North Island all year, but are only caught in the lower North and South Islands in summer when sea temperatures increase.

Temperature also triggers spawning. Snapper spawning generally occurs in spring; with other species, like trevally and gurnard, spawning generally happens during winter. When fish congregate to spawn they are a lot easier to target.

To use the sea temperatures to your advantage you need to know which species prefer what temperatures.

Swell: Swell is the lift in the ocean caused by air pressure and wind. The direction and height of swell can create some interesting fishing scenarios. The first point to think about is how the swell will affect the spot you're looking to fish. A rock ledge with a 3 m, onshore swell would be dangerous and should not be considered. A few days later the swell may have subsided to a safe level and fish will be in feeding in the well-oxygenated water on all the forage dislodged by the swell over the last few days.

Fishing inside headlands that have swell pushing past them can be very productive, especially if the swell is not from the usual direction. When current and swell oppose they can create pressure waves that push small fish and plankton to the surface where they're easy prey for larger fish. Swell height is featured in marine weather reports and should always be a consideration when choosing your spot.

Water conditions: Water conditions vary in many ways – clarity, sediment, oxygenation, freshwater run-off, natural phenomenon like algae blooms, or man-made influences like pollution. Conditions are usually easy to assess with a visual check.

Water conditions can work to your advantage. When fishing shallow water a bit of discolouration can help camouflage lines and hooks, whereas gin-clear water can make fish very spooky. Very still, calm water can be lacking in saturated oxygen and fish tend to avoid or not feed very actively in super-calm water.

Pollution can have an effect on fishing. When the grain boats offload their cargo around the Auckland wharves, the resultant spills act like a berley trail attracting snapper and trevally that would not normally be in the area. And obviously where bad pollution affects the natural ecosystem, the fishing is usually poor.

Wind: In most cases, wind is not the friend of the fisherman. Too much wind makes the sea rough and causes the boat to swing around on the anchor. To best use wind to your advantage, always try to get the wind and tide running in the same direction – for some reason the fishing is always better when you can do this.

The other way to use the wind to your advantage is to drift-fish when tide or currents are slack. This way you cover ground and experience the same effect as having a good current.

The ability to read weather maps and interpret marine weather forecasts will help immensely when learning how to pick a spot and predicting the conditions on the water.

Water safety

Take a commonsense approach with your fishing when it comes to water safety. **NO FISH IS WORTH DYING FOR.** Most people drown because they end up in the water unexpectedly. So expect at some stage to end up in the water.

The basic rules for boats:
1. Have the necessary skill and knowledge to safeguard everyone on board.
2. Make sure your vessel, and all of its equipment, is well maintained.
3. Carry all the right safety equipment.
4. Have a minimum of two means of communication – VHF radio, cellphone, flares, EPIRB.
5. Make sure everyone onboard has a correctly fitting life jacket, and if they are not competent swimmers, make sure they wear them at all times.

People risk their lives every day. All that is needed is a little common sense.

6. Make sure the weather conditions and forecast are suitable for the planned trip.
7. Know the maritime 'rules of the road'.
8. Do not overload your vessel and stow all equipment safely.
9. Tell someone where you are going and when you will be back.

When fishing from the shore:
1. Always check the weather before going rock fishing, especially swell forecasts. A rising swell with an incoming tide should be avoided.
2. Check the tides. Some good locations are completely covered when the tide is in, others just get cut off. Explore unfamiliar locations on an outgoing tide.
3. Assess the sea conditions before climbing down onto a ledge to fish. Spend at least 10 minutes watching the wave pattern. Don't stand on wet rocks when waves or spray are obviously sweeping them.
4. Don't fish alone! If possible, fish with someone who knows the area and can judge whether it is safe under the prevailing conditions.
5. If you're even a little uneasy about the fishing spot, find a safer place.
6. Keep well back from the water's edge, especially if there is a swell running.
7. Under no circumstances turn your back to the sea. Watch the waves at all times and be prepared to run to higher ground at any time.
8. Don't risk your life for your tackle or a fish. If you drop something, or a wave washes your gear into the sea, leave it there.

9. Wear suitable clothing. Good, non-slip, lace-up shoes or basketball boots are good. Don't wear gumboots.
10. Wear a buoyancy aid. Lightweight inflatable life jackets are suitable for fishing and are available in New Zealand.
11. Take notice of any warning signs – they're there for a reason.

Essential tools

The basic maps of areas have been provided as a guide and the icons denote whether a location is a boat, rock, beach or wharf fishing spot.

To get the most from this book, and to ensure safety, always use local maps and hydrographic charts, along with other navigational equipment.

Left: Fish finder.
Right: GPS.

Icons

These icons appear throughout the book to let you know what kind of fishing is recommended in the area.

Rocks	Wharf	Boat	Beach

Cape Reinga to Whangarei

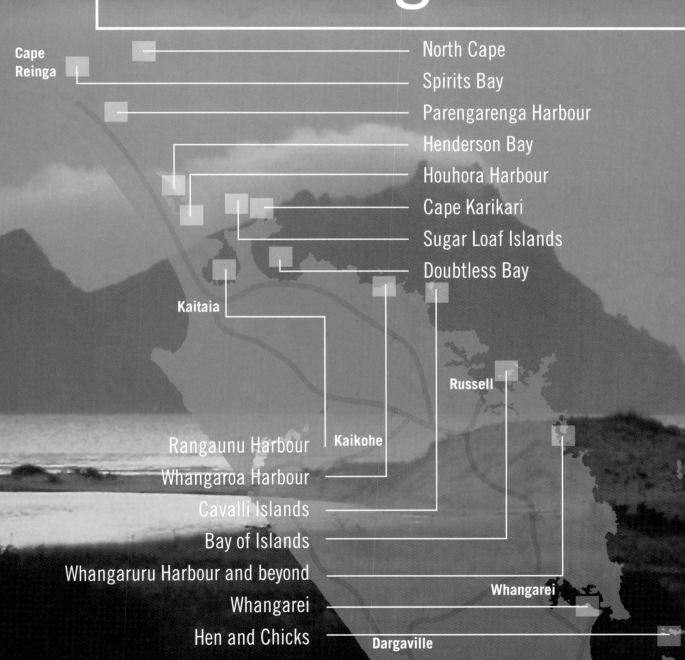

Cape Reinga

North Cape

Spirits Bay

Parengarenga Harbour

Henderson Bay

Houhora Harbour

Cape Karikari

Sugar Loaf Islands

Doubtless Bay

Kaitaia

Russell

Rangaunu Harbour

Kaikohe

Whangaroa Harbour

Cavalli Islands

Bay of Islands

Whangaruru Harbour and beyond

Whangarei

Whangarei

Hen and Chicks

Dargaville

North Cape

The northernmost tip of New Zealand offers anglers a variety of good fishing options. After exiting Parengarenga Harbour, turn left and head for the last point you can see – North Cape – it is about an 18 km run.

For trailer boats up to 6 m the easiest way to access 'The Cape' is by launching at Paua in Parengarenga Harbour. You will need to get a key from the Te Kao store to access the camping ground were the launching site is located.

The launch site is quite shallow and generally requires a 4WD vehicle. Larger vessels should launch at Houhora Harbour.

The best wind direction is westerly with a swell from the west. In good weather the whole area offers lots of fishing options; from drifting over the sand, trolling for gamefish and targeting hapuku in deep water to chasing big kingfish and snapper close to the rocks.

Big kingfish usually bite best from January through to May and can be found right on Murimotu, the island off the tip of North Cape, as well as off the ledges under the Surville Cliffs. There are some good underwater structures in this area and quality livebaits, such as kahawai and mackerel, fished on a deepwater rig, are very effective.

At times, kingfish will school up on the surface chasing baitfish. If you

This kahawai is hooked where it can swim freely – attracting the most attention.

come across this sort of action, jigging and popper fishing can be exciting. Snapper fishing can be approached in three ways. Around April/May, snapper school up over the sand in 30 m and drift-fishing with flasher rigs will turn up all the fish you want. September to December is the time to target trophy-sized fish. The best approach is to strayline right in close to the rocks with big baits rigged on 80 lb trace, no sinker and 8/0 circle hooks. Use kina for berley to really attract the big snapper to the area. The best bait is a whole mackerel or fresh mullet fillet.

Over summer you will find the snapper taking up residence on the reefs at a depth of 10–30 m. Anchoring over these structures and fishing with lightly weighted baits, such as pilchard and squid, will normally produce a feed. The fishing will generally be more productive when the tide is rising in the evening, as the fish can be shy during the heat of the day.

About 5 km offshore from North Cape is an ocean contour where the bottom falls away rapidly from 100 m. Drifting along the edge of this contour, especially if you can pick up where a finger of 100-m deep seafloor juts out into deeper water, can turn on some great fishing. You will need an excellent sounder and GPS to find this kind of structure. Looking for signs of fish at this depth and setting up the boat to drift the right direction can be tricky. Get it right though and you will catch hapuku and bluenose. Use a dropper rig baited with live mackerel or squid.

Best baits
Live koheru
Squid
Live kahawai
Pilchard

Recommended fishing gear
24 kg stand-up set
8/10 kg overhead set
60 kg trace
5/0 flasher rigs
10/0 livebaiting hooks
16 oz loop sinkers

The author with a nice snapper caught right under North Cape.

Spirits Bay

Located in the far north of the North Island, Spirits Bay is a spectacular bay with a pristine golden sand beach flanked by Spirits Mountain, or Kapowairua. To get there, head north on SH1 and turn right at Waitiki Landing, then follow the signposts down the gravel road to the camp ground.

The Spirits Bay camping ground has a small daily charge and basic facilities such as toilets and fresh water. During summer it gets busy, but after the peak holiday season you can have the place to yourself. Mosquitoes can be a problem, so a good repellent is necessary. The nearest shop is at Waitiki Landing 18 km away. It carries basic essentials and offers accommodation and fuel.

Best baits

Live kahawai
Pilchard
Skipjack
Piper
Mullet

Spirits Bay offers a variety of fishing – beach, rock and boat. The spot is probably best known for the huge kingfish that hunt the rock ledges at the right-hand end of the beach. The closest spot is called 'The Island' (Pananehe Island) and can be accessed easily at low tide. Fishing off the front or right-hand side of The Island is most productive. Walking past The Island takes you to the main ledges, which have restricted access due to tide and swell. Just past the ledge that has rod holders cemented into the rocks is a gut that cannot be crossed. This spot is called 'Rod Holders' and is famous for the large kingfish that have been landed there over the years.

A live kahawai rigged on a 10/0 hook and a 3 m, 60 kg trace suspended under a party balloon is the deadly rig for this spot. Rod Holders fishes best when the current is pushing right on the ledge. Large bronze whaler sharks often cruise these ledges and will take livebaits aimed at kingies. During the winter months large snapper and trevally can be caught by casting large unweighted baits off this ledge.

For the more adventurous, take a walk over the top of Spirits Mountain – it's about 20 minutes to the summit – and try dropping down on Hooper Point or one of the many other ledges. These offer the best fishing in the region and don't receive a lot of fishing pressure.

The beach itself offers productive fishing, especially at dawn and dusk. Look for any gutters offering slightly deeper water. This is best done at low tide by marking the spot with a stick in the sand above the high-water mark.

Kahawai, trevally and eagle rays are common; finding snapper can be a little trickier. They do come into the beach in good numbers at certain times, but there appears to be no pattern as to when or why.

In spring and summer school sharks or tope can be about in plague numbers off the beach, especially if you are fishing after dark. These sharks do provide good sport and are nice to eat if cleaned and prepared quickly after being caught.

When conditions suit, small boats can be dropped into the stream, and then dragged a short distance over the sand where the stream meets the sea to launch into the surf. The best boat fishing spot is the small rocky island in the middle of the bay. Kahawai, kingfish, trevally and snapper are the most commonly caught species.

Trolling small squid or feather jigs a few miles offshore in summer will produce skipjack tuna, or bonito as they are commonly called, which make excellent bait.

Recommended fishing gear
Surfcasting rig
15/24 kg livebaiting set-up
8/10 kg spinning outfit
Long rock gaff
60 kg trace
Large popper
10/0 livebaiting hooks
Onion sacks and ropes for berley
Break-out sinkers for beach fishing

Spirits Bay is famous for the kingfish that hunt around the rocks.

Parengarenga Harbour

New Zealand's northernmost harbour offers good shore-based and boat fishing. There are two main ways to access Parengarenga: off SH1F at Paua Road, which takes you to Paua Wharf, the camping ground and boat launching site, or turn right a few kilometres further up SH1F at Waitiki Landing. Follow the signs to Te Hapua.

In winter Paua offers large trevally that can be very challenging. To catch them requires the use of small baits and hooks with light traces, as they can be very timid biters. Once hooked, trevally will do everything in their power to bust you off on the wharf pilings.

Paua Wharf doesn't look much at first glance, but can produce awesome trevally and kingfish action.
Photo: Kent Fraser.

Just out from the boat launching spot is a shell bank. This is a great spot to fish out of a kayak or small boat. Kingfish, snapper and kahawai hunt on the edge of the channel. Casting freshly caught piper or livebaiting with kahawai produces large kingfish.

I remember a trip I had here with an American buddy. I had been talking up how good this area was. We had drawn a total blank at Spirits Bay and things were looking quiet in the harbour. After a while the kahawai started boiling off the corner of the shell bank and we quickly secured a couple using saltwater fly gear. When I told him they were actually the bait, he was speechless.

I quickly baited up one of the kahawai and had trolled it no more than 100 m along the bank when it was eaten by a kingfish of 25 kg. We quickly repeated this process with my buddy catching a kingfish of similar proportions.

Heading out from Te Kao Channel, the harbour has a hole of about 12 m. Anchoring in this hole on an incoming tide will produce good results any time of year. However, in summer the influx of school sharks can spoil your fishing.

At the mouth of Parengarenga Harbour are some boat wrecks. The ones on the southern side of the harbour are another hotspot for big trevally in winter and spring and kingfish and bronze whaler sharks in summer. Outgoing tide and calm conditions are best. Fish either the top or bottom of the outgoing tide as the currents here can become very strong and treacherous.

I have many fond memories of Te Hapua Wharf as it has been very productive for me over the years and it still continues to produce fish. You never know what kind of fishing to expect. Sometimes John dory will be everywhere. The local kids' technique for catching Johnnies is quite unique. They stand on the high wharf piles, and when a John dory is spotted, they bomb it by jumping on top of it. The stunned John dory is then caught by hand.

Because of the variety of fish that can be caught here, the best way to fish Te Hapua is with a couple of rigs. Use a surfcaster to fish the channel with a cut bait, plus a 10–15 kg rig with a live piper, sprat or yellowtail, all of which can be easily caught around Te Hapua Wharf, for bigger fish. Using this two-rod technique allows you to cover all your bases as different fish come on the bait at different times.

The rest of the Parengarenga Harbour is quite productive and it is always fun exploring the mangroves where you will find snapper and kahawai in very shallow water. Mullet and flounder can be found around the sandy flats.

The camping ground at Paua is basically a paddock, so take your own drinking water and a chemical toilet if you intend to camp here. The lack of facilities is more than made up for by the views of the silica sands and close access to the harbour.

Best baits
Live kahawai
Piper
Tuatua
Cubes of pilchard

Recommended fishing gear
Surfcasting rig
10/15 kg livebait outfit
40 kg trace
20 kg trace
Popper
40 g jigs
10/0 livebaiting hooks
4/0 suicide hooks

Catching piper is fun and they make great bait.

Henderson Bay

Henderson Bay is situated just north of Houhora. Boaties can launch at Houhora Harbour and shore-based fishermen can follow the signposts from SH1.

Best baits

Piper
Whole maomao
Skipjack tuna
Pilchard

Recommended fishing gear

Rock rods
10/15 kg jig outfit
40 kg trace
20 kg trace
10/0 livebaiting hooks
6/0 recurved hooks

A couple of good fishing options are available off Henderson Bay. In late November schools of snapper congregate in 35–50 m over the sand and areas of low foul off the bay. Using your sounder, either look for signs of fish activity or some likely looking structure to fish over. Drift-fishing can be highly productive when the winds are not too strong. The best rig to use is a 2 m, 10 kg-rated outfit rigged with a 5/0 flasher rig and a 6 oz sinker. Bait up with fresh skipjack tuna (bonito).

If the conditions are not suitable for drift-fishing, anchoring and fishing with big baits on a rig with up to three 2 oz ball sinkers rigged straight onto the hook works well. Vary your weight depending on the strength of the current.

A hot bait when the big fish are in is a whole maomao with the top and bottom fins trimmed off.

Grenville Point at the southern end of Henderson Bay can turn it on for shore-based anglers. It's a reasonable hike down to the point on soft sand, so travel light and carry a drink or two. The best conditions are after a bit of an onshore blow when things start to calm down. Good snapper, kingfish kahawai and trevally will come into a berley trail set off these rocks.

The best rigs for this spot are a 2.5 m rock rod with 15 kg line. Using unweighted or lightly weighted piper baits works really well.

Catching reef fish is a good sign that you are in the right area.

Houhora Harbour

Houhora Harbour is the ideal place to introduce kids to fishing as there are lots of areas to explore. The range of fishing options is huge in what is a relatively small harbour. The sheltered waters also make Houhora ideal for small boats. Fishing on the edges of channels and holes on a rising tide will provide a variety of fish, including some very large snapper.

The commercial wharf at Pukenui is a great place to catch sprats, piper and mackerel. These can be used as livebaits for the many John dory and big kingfish that patrol around the wharf in summer. The locals use heavy nylon hand-lines to pull the kingies away from the piles. The rig is baited with a live mackerel lowered to the bottom with a heavy sinker.

If you travel right up the harbour the flounder fishing is superb from November through to late January. Spearing at night is the favoured method, although a well placed net will also provide good results.

Surfcasting at the heads on the eastern side of the harbour can produce excellent fishing at times. The trick is to use hard baits like octopus or kahawai to avoid the pickers.

Out from the entrance, quite strong currents attract predators that feed on baitfish on the outgoing tide. Trolling with a large lure or live kahawai will often produce kingfish action.

Bottom fishing in 30 to 40 m from late March through to May produces some of the best snapper fishing you could wish for. Finding them is usually a matter of working outwards from the heads to East Beach to the south. Drift-fishing over the sand works well in this area.

Houhora Harbour is a protected harbour with safe anchorages for large launches and good launching ramps. There is plenty of accommodation and facilities, but it pays to book as during holiday periods things get pretty busy.

Best baits

Kahawai, used live or as cut bait
Pilchard
Live mackerel
Piper
Octopus

Recommended fishing gear

Surfcasting rig
6–8 kg boat set
15 kg heavy boat set
Trolling lures, diving minnows in large sizes
60 kg trace
20 kg trace
10/0 livebaiting hooks
4/0 suicide hooks
4/0 flasher rigs
Bait sabikis
Break-out sinkers for beach fishing

Hard baits like fresh squid work well on big snapper around Houhora.

Moturoa/Sugar Loaf Islands

The Moturoa/Sugar Loaf Islands lie north of Cape Karikari and offer good all-round fishing for most species. These islands are definitely big fish country. Livebaiting here could produce anything from a monster snapper to a marlin, so whatever you do, make sure you use tackle that will cope with larger fish. A 24 kg game rig is recommended.

Access is easiest by launching at Matai Bay or Rangiputa. A 4WD is required for both areas. Check weather conditions carefully and use a 5.5 m plus boat for offshore fishing.

Best baits

Live kahawai
Live koheru
Squid
Mullet
Jack mackerel
Piper

Recommended fishing gear

10–15 kg straylining set
24 kg heavy game set
100 kg trace
40 kg trace
12/0 circle hooks
8/0 suicide hooks
2 oz ball sinkers
Good gaff
Large landing net

Sometimes it pays to fish heavy tackle in tiger country.

To target big snapper, anchor so that you are facing a gutter or headland and cast big baits such as whole jack mackerel and piper into the shallow

wash. Don't use any sinker, just a large unweighted bait. Big snapper hang around these washes; they like to feed on the many kina that live there. Berleying with smashed up kina is a very effective way to attract snapper.

Kingfish hunt out from the main islands around and over the pinnacles of rock. Fishing with live koheru over the pinnacles using a 12/0 circle hook and 100 kg trace should do the job.

Rangaunu Harbour

If you turn off SH10 at Cape Karikari, you'll see a shallow harbour flanked by golden sand dunes. Strong currents have cut many channels and at the top end mangroves grow freely.

Because of the shallow nature of the harbour, the currents are often swift, so large sinkers may be required to combat the effects of the current, particularly when fishing at the entrance. Using a dropper rig with teardrop sinker is ideal when the current is at its strongest.

Channel markers and buoys in the harbour provide good fishing for kingfish. Casting or trolling is the most effective way to target them and the best time of year is from January through to the end of May.

One of the prime species in Rangaunu Harbour is trevally. They tend

The best boat launching is at Rangiputa on the eastern side of the harbour or Kaimaumau on the west. 4WDs are required for launching. There is plenty of good accommodation in this region from basic camping grounds to deluxe resorts. The local general store stocks all food and bait requirements.

Best baits
Fresh tuatua
Mussel
Live kahawai
Squid
Mullet

Recommended fishing gear
8–10 kg straylining set
15 kg trolling set
20 kg trace
15 kg trace
6/0 circle hooks
3/0 suicide hooks
6 oz teardrop sinkers
2 oz ball sinker

to school in late winter and early spring and for some reason they seem to grow very big here – specimens as big as 8 kg have been recorded. The best way to catch them is to fish off the sand banks using shellfish for bait. Trevally can be finicky biters so use small, strong hooks to catch them and keep your trace as light as possible.

Rangaunu Harbour can produce XOS trevally. This is an average size fish for the area. Photo: Cecil Alexander.

Cape Karikari

Cape Karikari offers access to deep water straight off the cape. The fishing options are endless with many rocky headlands and offshore reefs.

Gamefish such as marlin and tuna come close to shore and are accessible to small boat anglers. Large kingfish and snapper hunt the washes off the headlands.

One of the best spots to look for snapper is called Knuckle Point. The fish seem to move in at dawn and dusk. Anchoring close to the rocks and using lots of ground bait is the best method.

From late December onwards, trolling with small pink squid lures a few miles offshore in the bluewater will produce skipjack tuna. These fish make fantastic bait for snapper. They also provide a great introduction to sportfishing. Use 6 kg to 8 kg tackle and you'll have a ball.

There are some areas of low-lying reef structures in 60 to 80 m of water that produce tarakihi and hapuku around October. Using a fishfinder and GPS is the only way to find these spots unless you have the locals' marks and a good chart. These deep reefs fish best on the rising tide when the moon is waning.

Fishing for hapuku in shallow water can be really exciting. The best rig is a heavy dropper tied with 100 kg trace and two 11/0 circle hooks. Baits of fresh skipjack or barracouta are good.

At the base of the peninsula is Whatuwhiwhi, which is a good place to launch small boats and fish inshore snapper off the back of Tokerau Beach. This area is very sheltered if the wind is from the northwesterly quarter.

Camping grounds and accommodation are plentiful in this area, as are fuel and supplies. It is a popular holiday destination and can get crowded over Christmas and New Year.

Best baits

Fresh skipjack
Live kahawai
Barracouta
Mullet
Squid

Recommended fishing gear

10–15 kg straylining set
6–8 kg jig set
24 kg heavy game set
100 kg trace
40 kg trace
9/0 short-shank livebait hooks
5 cm pink squid lures
8/0 suicide hooks
1 oz ball sinkers

Launch in the corner of the bay at Whatuwhiwhi.

Doubtless Bay

Doubtless Bay stretches from Berghan Point in the south to Cape Karikari in the north. The standout feature of Doubtless Bay is its numerous exposed reefs, the best two being Fairway Reef and Albert Reef.

I remember one fishing session with friends at Fairway Reef. We had netted some fresh mullet from the Taipa River and every bait was nailed by a snapper of at least 5 kg (11 lb) and many were close to 9 kg (20 lb). All of us were constantly hooked up to fish for over five hours. It was some of the finest snapper fishing I have ever experienced.

All of the reefs in the bay provide excellent fishing action. The best way to fish them is to anchor close and use straylining tackle. Groundbait will definitely attract the fish to your boat. It pays to put out a livebait as well as fishing on the bottom, as many predators hang around the reef.

The rocks from Coopers Beach right through to the beginning of Tokerau Beach provide fine platforms for surfcasters and rock fishermen who can expect to catch snapper, kahawai, trevally and kingfish. The best time to fish these platforms is in the early morning or late afternoon. Fishing appears to be better when the moon is low. There is no need to cast a long way, as the fish tend to hang close to the rocks. A standard running rig with a 2 oz sinker is the ideal rig for this area.

Mangonui Harbour fishes really well for snapper and the commercial wharf is famous for its kingfish and John dory. You can catch John dory all year round and kingfish over summer.

The wharf is a great place to catch fresh bait such as yellowtail and slimy mackerel. Use a light spinning rod and a set of sabikis tipped with a little bait to catch these baitfish. Employ the same rig for kingfish as you would for John dory with a livebait and a running sinker set on the bottom.

At times pilchards school in Mangonui Harbour and when this happens the fishing is superb. You can catch pilchards with sabikis and use them as livebait or dead bait.

Berghan Point offers access to very deep water close to shore. Here you can expect to catch tarakihi and kingfish close to the point, and if you move offshore little, you'll find some hapuku grounds. You'll need a chart or GPS to locate the right area.

This is also a good spot to troll for yellowfin tuna and billfish, as the bluewater currents push right in here in summer.

There are boat ramps at Mangonui Harbour and in the Taipa River. Launching is best done over the top of the tide. Try the awesome fish and chips at the Mangonui Fish shop.

Best baits

Jack mackerel
Fresh mullet
Live slimy mackerel
Piper
Mullet

Recommended fishing gear

10–15 kg straylining set
3/0 flashers
24 kg heavy game set
24 kg trace
100 kg trace
9/0 short-shank livebait hooks
5/0 suicide hooks
Size 14 sabikis
1 oz ball sinkers

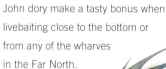
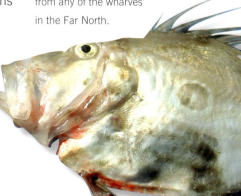

John dory make a tasty bonus when livebaiting close to the bottom or from any of the wharves in the Far North.

Whangaroa Harbour

Whangaroa Harbour is flanked by impressive cliffs and has a narrow entrance. It offers plenty of safe anchorages for big boats. The upper part of the harbour can produce a mixture of snapper, kahawai and trevally. This harbour is also a great spot for small boats. Use light tackle because, generally, the fish are not large.

There are two wharves, one for the gamefishing boats, and a commercial wharf. The John dory fishing off the commercial wharf is excellent. Use live sprats for bait, rigged on a dropper with a 4 oz sinker.

There are some good scallop beds around the island at the top of the harbour.

At the entrance to the harbour is a headland called Kingfish Point. Drift-fishing past this point with livebait on the bottom can produce exciting results. Spring and early summer is usually the best time to try.

When conditions allow, taking small boats around the corner at the entrance to the harbour to the rocks to the north will produce excellent snapper fishing in-close with unweighted baits.

Offshore a few miles are Stephenson Island and Stephenson Reef. Both spots offer good snapper, tarakihi and kingfish fishing. High-speed jigging for kingfish on Stephenson Reef can be really good. Use 200 g jigs dropped to the bottom and wound back to the surface as fast as you can. When the fish are there, you'll see them chasing the jigs to the surface. This is really exciting fishing, which I have experienced many times, catching kingfish up to 24 kg.

To get to Whangaroa, turn off SH10 just past Kaeo. There is accommodation in the form of motor camps, campsites, cabins and hotels. At the entrance to the harbour is Kingfish Lodge, which offers upmarket accommodation. This lodge is only accessible by boat.

Recommended fishing gear

10–l5 kg light game set
6–10 kg jig set
4/0 flasher rigs
150 g jigs
24 kg trace
100 kg trace
8/0 livebait hooks
6–8 oz tear drop sinkers

Best baits

Pilchard
Live koheru
Piper
Skipjack
Squid

Cavalli Islands

The Cavalli Islands are famous for the wreck of the *Rainbow Warrior*, sunk here as an artificial reef after it was bombed by French terrorists in Auckland in 1985.

The best way to get to the Cavalli Islands is by beach launching off Matauri Bay. The road to the bay is signposted from SH10. A 4WD or tractor is a necessity for beach launching here.

Fishing around the islands can be very productive. To catch snapper, fish back into the wash off the islands.

Motutapere Island is the northernmost of the group. Here you will find schools of koheru that can be caught on baitfish jigs. If you livebait with these close to the islands, there is a good chance of catching a large kingfish.

At the southern end of Motukawanui Island, the largest in the group, is a point that is also good for targeting kingfish. Here the preferred technique is to troll with live kahawai.

Just out from the islands a few miles is the Taheke Reef. This spot offers a wide variety of species, including snapper, golden snapper, tarakihi and kingfish. The best way to fish here is with either baited flasher rigs or jigs. Fishing off the edge of the reef or where schooling fish are located are the best options. This area can also produce yellowfin tuna, striped marlin and mako sharks.

The diving is also very good. The wreck of the *Rainbow Warrior* offers a good scenic dive and diving close to the islands will produce scallops and crayfish.

There is a large camping ground at Matauri Bay, but it pays to be fully self-sufficient once you're there.

Best baits
Live koheru
Live kahawai
Piper
Skipjack
Squid
Pilchard

Recommended fishing gear
10–15 kg jig set
8–10 kg boat set
90 g jigs
24 kg trace
100 kg trace
4/0 flashers
10/0 livebait hooks

A seafood smorgasbord caught around the Cavalli Islands.

Bay of Islands

The Bay of Islands is a well-known hotspot for fishermen. The gamefishing was made famous by Zane Grey and 'The Bay' continues to fish well to this day.

There is plenty of accommodation to suit every budget and good facilities all around the Bay of Islands. It is still possible to camp on some of the islands — you may require permission from DOC or the owners.

The opportunities to catch good fish are present throughout the year. It would be hard to name all the good spots in the Bay of Islands, as it would take a lifetime to fish them all. What I have done is isolate the better spots, but you'll still have to look around to find exactly where the fish are.

The Hole in the Rock at Cape Brett.

Starting at the northern end of the bay is Nine Pin Rock. Fishing with a dropper rig and circle hooks baited with live mackerel will produce kingfish, snapper and John dory. There are normally schools of maomao, trevally and kahawai at the Nine Pin — use these schools to guide you as to where to fish or use your fishfinder to look for bottom structure or fish sign near the bottom.

Cape Brett and Piercy Island, famous for the Hole in the Rock, are good spots to bottom-fish for snapper and trevally. Fish here with a two-hook dropper rig or strayline with large baits, as sometimes the larger fish patrol in mid-water. Better still, employ both techniques at once. There's always an opportunity to catch a big kingfish here by jigging or livebaiting in-close to Piercy Island. There is a rise at the back of Cape Brett where the water comes up to 100 m. This spot is good for hapuku fishing and jigging for kingfish. It's clearly marked on all marine charts.

Bird Rock offers fishing similar to Cape Brett's. The best spot is the reef that comes up about half a kilometre off the rock on the northern side.

In late October and early November large snapper start to school off the area around Red Head, Mita's Foul and out over the Middle Foul. When the fish move in, catching a snapper of 9 kg (20 lb) to 15 kg (33 lb) is not uncommon. Fishing with standard straylining and bottom-fishing techniques works well. But a word of caution: it is easy to remove a lot of prime breeding fish from the biomass when this type of fishing occurs. I stress conservation and catch-and-release – take only enough to eat or one big fish as a trophy.

There are plenty of rock platforms, beaches and wharves to suit land-based fishermen. The close spots like Tapeka Point and Rawhiti can fish well, or if you like hiking, take a walk over to Whangamumu, visit the old whaling station and fish off the rocks on the right-hand side of the point. The walk will take about an hour if you're fit.

The spots I have mentioned here barely scratch the surface of what is available in the Bay of Islands. It is a beautiful place to explore and fish, and I've never been disappointed with the results. I caught my first 9 kg (20lb) plus snapper in a few metres of water beside Roberton Island, on a day when the weather limited the fishing options, and have had many great fishing adventures in 'The Bay' since.

Best baits
Live koheru
Live kahawai
Piper
Skipjack
Squid
Pilchard

Recommended fishing gear
10–15kg boat set
8–10 kg jig set
150 g jigs
24 kg trace
100 kg trace
8/0 suicide hooks
10/0 livebait hooks
6 to 8 oz teardrop sinkers

I like to release big snapper. This one was about 10 kg.

Whangaruru Harbour and beyond

Heading up SH1 north of Whangarei is a turnoff at Whakapara that takes you to Whangaruru Harbour. While the harbour itself does not offer outstanding fishing, the outlying waters are very productive.

There are camping grounds and basic cabins at Whangaruru and Bland Bay. There is reasonable boat launching off the beach and from the ramp in the harbour.

Best baits

Live koheru
Piper
Pilchard

Recommended fishing gear

24 kg heavy game set
10–15 kg jig set
24 kg trace
150 kg trace
10/0 livebait hooks
5/0 suicide hooks
7–10 g jigs

One of the best spots is Danger Rock. Once you get outside the harbour you should be able to see the rock, or use a chart for navigation.

Danger Rock is actually two rocks, which are exposed at all times. Good schools of kingfish and kahawai patrol around these rocks. Trolling, jigging and livebaiting all work very well.

Using 7 to 10 g jigs on what would be the shadowy side of the reef will produce large koheru, which make excellent cut and livebaits. It pays to use heavy tackle for livebaiting here for two reasons. One, the kingfish try to bust you off on the reef, which is very close; and two, several black marlin have been hooked while livebaiting here.

Inshore and to the north is Home Point. Casting unweighted baits into the wash around the point can produce some excellent snapper. Anchoring and straylining amongst the broken rocks close to shore is also a good proposition.

Soft plastic lures work well fished down a berley trail.

Whangarei

Whangarei offers both harbour and shore fishing. A good run of trevally happens on the south corner off Ruakaka Beach in early spring. Surfcasting using tuatua and pilchards with small strong hooks is the only way to catch these fish.

In early summer, schools of snapper enter the harbour to spawn. Many of these fish are of only average size, but you will get the occasional big one. The best times to target these fish are late afternoon or early morning on the edges of the channels or over shellfish beds.

Near the harbour heads and along the main navigation channel are lots of navigation buoys. Casting poppers, jigs and piper close to these structures will attract strikes from kingfish, which vary in size from a couple of kilos up to 25 kg. The best approach is to let the current carry your drifting boat past the buoys, casting as you go. When you hook up, try to lead the fish away from the buoys, otherwise it will break you off around the buoy's mooring chain.

Just around from the heads to the north there are several good headlands. The first is called Busby Head. This is an excellent spot to troll livebaits or lures close to the rocks as big kingfish hang out here. The top of the tide and outgoing is usually when they're feeding.

Outside the heads and a bit further to the north is Bream Head, which

There are several launching ramps around Whangarei Harbour. One of the best is at One Tree Point in Ruakaka. You can launch boats to 6 m with a normal car, providing you have more than half-tide. You will need a tractor or 4WD vehicle at other times. Accommodation is plentiful around Whangarei and Ruakaka. Bookings are essential during holiday periods.

Kent Fraser with a nice gurnard caught on a flasher rig while drift-fishing.

Best baits

Tuatua
Piper
Pilchard

Recommended fishing gear

8 kg strayline set
10–15 kg jig set
24 kg trace
15 kg trace
4/0 flasher rigs
3/0 suicide hooks
Poppers

has a large reef coming out of about 50 m of water. This is a good spot to target tarakihi and snapper, with the occasional kingfish showing up for good measure.

Try using flasher rigs baited with squid or tuatua. Drift-fishing in about 40 m in this area can produce some good gurnard and snapper in winter and early spring.

If you travel by car out to Whangarei Heads you will arrive at Ocean Beach. Surfcasting for kahawai in the breakers can be a lot of fun and if you walk to the rocks to the right of the beach there is a gutter between two rocks that produces some big snapper. Use large unweighted baits like fillets of kahawai.

Bream Head – a good spot for tarakihi and snapper.

Hen and Chicks

The group of islands that is clearly visible when you leave Whangarei Harbour is called the Hen and Chickens. This group offers spectacular and varied fishing.

Straylining for large snapper at change of light in-close to the islands' many points and reefs can be very productive. Be sure to use plenty of berley and large fresh baits like mackerel and mullet fillets.

Moving off the islands and drifting over the foul in 30 to 50 m will produce plenty of good snapper and tarakihi. The trick here is to make sure that there is not too much breeze, and that your baits are kept close to the bottom.

You will need a 5 m plus boat to fish the Hen and Chicks unless the weather is perfect as it's a fair run back to shore and it can cut up very quickly here. In good conditions there are a few spots to anchor overnight.

Best baits
Tuatua
Piper
Pilchard

The Hen and Chickens Islands.

Use your sounder to find the bricks that are holding fish, as fish move around quite a lot with tide and current. Kingfish are always in residence around the islands, especially where the reefs fall away into deep water. Fishing with large live kahawai and koheru close to these ledges and points can be spectacular. Often, massive schools of kingfish hunt around the islands and can be spotted when they smash baitfish on the surface. When you see this action it's a good time to drop a large jig to the bottom and retrieve flat-out.

The large spire that can be seen to the south is Sail Rock. Bottom-fishing around this rock will produce everything from huge snapper to reef

Recommended fishing gear

8 kg strayline set
10–15 kg jig set
24 kg trace
15 kg trace
4/0 flasher rigs
3/0 suicide hooks
Poppers

fish and tarakihi. Kingfish in good numbers also call the rock home. The best way to fish Sail Rock is to drop a berley bomb down deep and fish with 2/0 flasher rigs baited with tuatua and squid. At the same time, cast lightly-weighted baits out the back of the boat. Often you will find the best snapper in mid-water.

During the warmer months of January to April gamefish like skipjack, yellowfin tuna, mako sharks and marlin are present in the blue water off the back of the islands. The area between the Hen and Chicks, Mokohinau Islands and Little Barrier Island is known as the Golden Triangle. Trolling livebaits and lures on big game tackle is worth the effort when the water temperature is between 19 and 22°C.

Ninety Mile Beach
to Kaipara

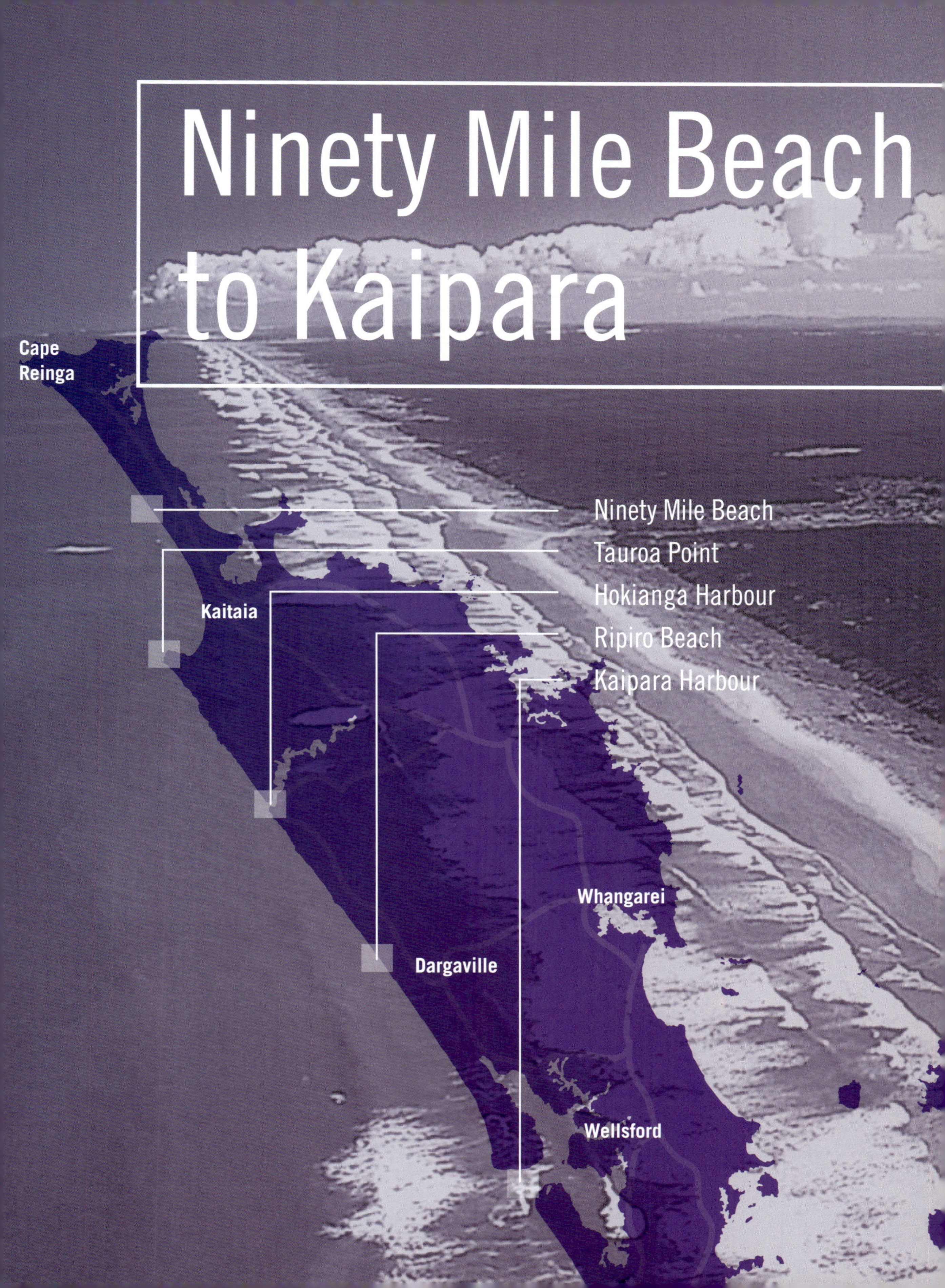

Cape
Reinga

Kaitaia

Ninety Mile Beach

Tauroa Point

Hokianga Harbour

Ripiro Beach

Kaipara Harbour

Whangarei

Dargaville

Wellsford

Ninety Mile Beach

The 'Ninety' is a vast expanse of beach located on the west coast of the far north of the North Island. Ironically, Ninety Mile Beach is only around 56 miles (90 kilometres) long and is classified as a highway where all the rules of the road apply. It is used by tourist operators, land yachts and fishermen.

You can access Ninety Mile Beach at Ahipara, Waipapakauri and Te Paki Stream. You can travel safely at low tide in most 4WD vehicles. There is good accommodation and camp sites at Waipapakauri. You should always book over summer and when the big surfcasting competition is on in early March.

The beach starts at Ahipara in the south and runs continuously to Te Paki Stream in the north.

Ninety Mile Beach can seem like a desert to the uninitiated. In fact it is a true oasis, with vast shellfish beds that are exposed at low water, huge stingrays working behind the breakers feeding on crabs and lots of fish moving into the gutters formed by the west coast waves.

Many anglers take up the challenge of landing snapper off the beach. I also find targeting the more common species like trevally, kahawai and gurnard to be very rewarding.

While the beach is a constantly changing environment that can make finding the fish tough, there are a few tricks to success.

If the swell is more than 2 m high, it can be too rough and dangerous. Leave it for another day.

Before actually wetting a line, take a drive up the beach at low tide to identify potential gutters and holes that may be worth fishing. These spots can be shown up by a secondary wave break or an area of deeper-looking water where the waves flatten out.

Look for spots to fish at different stages of the tide, as the tide will push you out of spots as it comes in and holes and gutters dry up as it recedes. Look, too, for an easterly weather pattern with a dropping swell – this will allow you to cast into the best gutters and holes. Fish definitely move in closer to shore at dawn and dusk. Wear a pair of wetsuit bottoms because wading is important to reach some spots.

Rigs must include break-out sinkers, which hold in the sand. If you use ordinary sinkers, your line will be swept up the beach.

Gathering bait can be as simple as collecting tuatua on the beach at low tide, which make excellent bait. Other good baits are squid, pilchard and octopus tentacle (skinned). Try to avoid big, bloody baits, as school sharks and rays can become a nuisance. Finally, always tie your bait on with bait elastic or cotton.

There are a couple of defined spots on the Ninety that are worth trying when the conditions are right. Three-quarters of the way up the beach is a large mussel-covered rock called 'The Bluff'. When the sea is calm, fishing off the front of the rock will produce awesome trevally action. Best fished for right at your feet, these tough fish will do their best to bust you off on the reef. Fish for them with strong line and small, strong hooks baited with shellfish.

Drive to the northern end of the beach and after a bit of a hike you will come to a rock ledge called Scott Point. Again, this spot is only worthwhile when the conditions are calm, as the ledge has claimed more than one victim. When the conditions are right, snapper fishing here is great.

If you are planning a holiday to fish Ninety Mile Beach, the best time is in March and April, as conditions are most settled and easterly weather patterns are common. Allow a week to find the fish and to experience ideal conditions.

Recommended fishing gear
4–5 m surf rod
Beach spike rodholder
Break-out sinkers
Bait cotton
Wetsuit
24 kg trace
4/0 hooks
3/0 suicide hooks

The best baits
Tuatua
Octopus
Pilchard

Ninety Mile Beach.
Photo: Destination Northland.

Tauroa Point

Tauroa Peninsula forms the southern end of Ninety Mile Beach. The extensive rocky tidal platform found at Tauroa Point is completely different terrain to the long, sandy beaches to the north. Access is best gained by 4WD or quad bike. Take the road from Ahipara to Shipwreck Bay.

Shipwreck Bay can be worth fishing if the swell is rising, as it does get some protection in a south-westerly wind.

Recommended fishing gear

10–15 kg rock rod
3 m gaff
24 kg trace
6/0 hooks
3/0 suicide hooks

The best baits

Pilchard
Mullet
Tuatua

The area is a popular fishing spot of the locals, as it is home to crayfish, paua and mussels that can be gathered on snorkel at low water when the sea is calm. This spot is best approached as a rock spot, as opposed to a surfcasting spot, so use 10–15 kg line and a rod with a fair bit of backbone to lift fish onto the ledge. A gaff with a 3 m pole can be very useful here, as I have seen some big fish lost close to the rocks.

Large trevally, kahawai and kingfish can be caught right off the ledge, while snapper and school sharks are usually caught by casting 50–80 m out.

At the northern side of the point, the land rises steeply from a narrow coastal flat that fronts the tidal platform. As you travel south around the point, the land becomes less steep and the fishing is not as productive.

Pipis make great bait for trevally.

Hokianga Harbour

The Hokianga includes the twin settlements of Omapere and Opononi, made famous in 1955–56 by Opo the dolphin. This is a really nice holiday destination with the charms of an area that is not overdeveloped.

There are two boat ramps, both of which are easy to access. It takes about 10 minutes from launching your boat to reach the Hokianga Bar, which at times can be extremely dangerous. Always cross the bar at the top of the tide when the current is slowest. If you are unfamiliar with the local conditions, contact Omapere Base (channel 88). They will be able to assist you.

As Hokianga is a west coast harbour, easterly winds and swell below 1.5 m are the conditions to look for. Once outside you will find a wide variety of species, including snapper, kingfish, blue cod, gurnard, trevally and kahawai. The best rigs to use are either dropper rigs or 5/0 flashers. The best way to find fish is to move into 35 m and drift-fish, but if you locate any structure, anchor on it. Cray pots can be good indicators.

Large numbers of gamefish are also caught in water betwen 50 and 100 m deep straight out from the bar. If the bar is too rough, the harbour itself is a pleasant spot to fish. Expect a few surprises. When mullet are schooling, trolling lures around the heads or livebaiting off the rock ledges will provide good action with kingfish. Fishing the edges of the channels up into the harbour will produce snapper, trevally and kahawai. There are a few wharves where it's worth chucking out a bait on a surfcaster for a kahawai or trevally while the kids are entertained catching sprats.

The best fishing is on the rising tide or the start of the outgoing tide – when the current really starts ripping the fishing can go quiet.

Three hours' drive north of Auckland on State Highway 12, the Hokianga has a wide range of accommodation to suit all budgets. Options include bed and breakfasts, farm stays, backpackers' lodges and camping grounds, as well as hotels and motels.

There is plenty to see, do and explore, including pony trekking, craft trails, wood carving, bush walks, sand dunes, swimming, golf, museums, great food at numerous cafes and eating establishments, or just taking it easy in a wonderful, relaxed atmosphere.

Recommended fishing gear
6–8 kg boat set
15 kg heavy boat set
Trolling lures, diving minnows in large sizes
60 kg trace
20 kg trace
10/0 livebaiting hooks
4/0 suicide hooks
4/0 flasher rigs

The best baits
Mullet
Salted bonito
Pilchard
Squid

Omapere Wharf in the Hokianga Harbour. Photo: Destination Northland.

Ripiro Beach

Ten minutes' drive from Dargaville is Baylys Beach, which is situated on the 100 km long Ripiro Ocean Beach. The beach is backed by high, golden sand dunes and is the site of many shipwrecks.

Baylys Beach is a small seaside community. For accommodation, use the internet search "Baylys Beach Accommodation". There are restaurants, where you can enjoy excellent meals, 4x4 quad bikes are available for hire to ride along the beach and surfcasting tours can also be arranged.

Ripiro Ocean Beach is New Zealand's longest drivable beach and is longer than the more famous Ninety Mile Beach. It is well worth the drive just for the experience.

The entrance at Baylys Beach is the most commonly used and consequently the whole beach is commonly known as Baylys Beach. The beach is a highway and the standard rules of the road apply. It is possible to drive along its hard sands two hours either side of low tide – 4WD vehicles are recommended. Ask locals about the conditions before venturing onto the sand.

You can gather tuatua all year round, but be careful not to be confused by the much larger toheroa that this area is also famous for. Toheroa are usually found higher up the beach and have a distinctive black tinge to their shell. You are not allowed to take toheroa under any circumstances – they are fully protected and there is no open season.

Like many of the west coast beaches there can be a lot of barren areas for fishermen, although anglers putting out kites and kontiki long-lines

The toheroa is fully protected and cannot be taken under any circumstances.

when the wind is in the east will be rewarded with catches of gurnard, kahawai and snapper. There is also good netting for mullet and flounder.

There are a couple of landmarks worth noting where surf fishermen enjoy good success. Maunganui Bluff, at the northern end of the beach, can produce prolific numbers of kahawai – trevally make up the balance of the catch. Although there are times when good snapper are caught here, it is not a spot where you will consistently catch them.

At the southern end, the beach swings into the Kaipara Harbour. This stretch of beach would have to be the most productive for surf anglers, with most species abundant here. Fishing on the bottom of the tide up to the first two hours of the incoming is normally the best, especially if this coincides with dawn or dusk. The currents here can be dramatic, so it's best to fish when the tidal range is low.

At the very southern end of Ripiro Beach is Pouto Point. This point faces back into the Kaipara Harbour and is about an hour's drive from Dargaville. Pouto Point is a great spot to target kingfish from the shore. From late November onwards, when the mullet and flounder enter the harbour, kingfish are usually not far behind. The best way to target them is with either a live or dead fresh mullet suspended beneath a party balloon. Note: I stressed fresh, as frozen baits do not hold the same appeal.

The next-best bait would be a live kahawai fished in the same manner. Many old-timers have told me live flounder fished on the bottom work very well for kingfish-bait, and I have opened up kingies that have been feeding on flounder.

If you can't get your hands on any livebait it is worth casting a large popper around the currents if you see any action.

The best baits
Mullet
Salted bonito
Pilchard
Squid

Recommended fishing gear
Kontikis or fishing kites
4–5 m surfcasting set
30 kg trace
10/0 livebaiting hooks
4/0 suicide hooks
Break-out sinkers

Flounder is a good alternative bait for kingfish in west coast harbours.

Kaipara Harbour

The Kaipara Harbour is the largest harbour in the Southern Hemisphere and there are dozens of boat ramps and wharves dotted around its shores. Of these, the best access from Auckland would be Shelly Beach, lying a bit over an hour north of Auckland. Follow State Highway 16 from Parakai and take a left. Look for the signs about 20 minutes past this point.

The Kaipara has many holiday areas dotted all around the harbour with camping grounds, accommodation, boat ramps and shops. The tide can go out a long way here so take this into account when launching boats. Caution should also be used when boating anywhere in the Kaipara as it can cut up rough when wind opposes tide.

The best baits
Mullet
Salted bonito
Pilchard
Squid
Crab

Recommended fishing gear
4–5 m surfcasting set
15 kg boat set with super braid
3/0 flasher rigs
20 kg trace
50 kg trace
10/0 livebaiting hooks
4/0 suicide hooks
Break-out sinkers
600 g leads
Flounder light
Flounder spear

Fishing can be split into inner harbour and outer harbour, inner being almost to Pouto Point, outer being the Graveyard and beyond.

The Graveyard is the area extending from the seaward, or western, side of Pouto out through the heads. As the name denotes, the Graveyard is home to many shipwrecks and maritime disasters. The fishing is very good, but this is a spot where extreme care must be exercised as the reputation is well-founded. It is sensible to go with someone who is familiar with the area or go with one of the charter boats that work the Kaipara.

The Graveyard has very strong currents and local fishermen often employ heavy handlines with sinkers up to 2 kg. This method is very effective.

Another option is to rig a 15 kg boat set with superbraid line and 600 g of lead. That's usually enough to get you to the bottom and catching fish. The two-hook dropper rig is definitely the best rig to use in the strong currents, as it makes bite detection easier and is less likely to tangle.

The Kaipara can be treacherous.

When the fishing is 'on' at the Graveyard, it's not uncommon to see snapper of 5–10 kg coming over the side, two at a time!

Due to the vast expanse of the inner Kaipara and its shallow nature, fish do move around quite a bit. The most common species are kahawai, gurnard and snapper. Some spots will produce more of one species than another, mainly due to the terrain. The smoother the bottom, the more gurnard. Rocky reef areas hold more snapper.

The best way to target snapper and gurnard is to work the edges of the sandbars and channels. Any spot where the depth increases quickly or there is a substantial structure like rocks, headlands and reefs is always worth looking for.

A word about current. Try to get the current and the wind moving in the same direction. This can mean moving depending on the tide.

In summer, the Kaipara is a nursery for many species, so it is common to encounter a lot of small fish in the calmer, shallow waters. These juveniles attract a lot of predators. Many species of shark, including white pointers and bronze whalers, spawn in the shallow waters.

When the mullet are schooling kingfish chase them in large numbers. High-speed jigging under working birds, or where there is visible surface activity, is very effective. This activity is normally found where the Tauhoa and Otamatea Channels meet.

A tip here is when one of the crew hooks a fish, get them to leave the fish in the water until another is hooked, as kingfish will stay with the hooked fish. This way you can stay on the school longer, rather than having to find them again.

Shellfish are abundant all around the Kaipara. Cockles and pipis can be found on most beaches at the low-water mark. Huge mussel beds can be found around any reef and scallops are located on the sandy areas along the edges of channels. Many of the fish species feed on these shellfish so they are a good indicator of where to fish.

The many wharves around the Kaipara make great spots for kids to fish for small fish and are also good for a bit of surfcasting, especially at night. If you use crab for bait you will catch plenty of dogfish, which make great eating. Use shellfish, and trevally will bite, or salted skipjack for gurnard and snapper.

The Kaipara is full of flounder and spearing in the calm bays at night is always worth a try. The water must be clear to spot these tasty little flatfish. Make sure you have a rising tide around 10pm. Wading very slowly on the edge of the waterline and in the shallows on incoming tide is the way to hunt flounder. The best lights to use are the ones you hold underwater, as they reduce the surface glare and make it far easier to spot your prey.

For the hardcore surfcaster, South Head has a large lagoon that is sheltered from the west coast swell by a long sandbar. To get there you have to drive up Muriwai Beach from the Rimmers Road crossing, which is located on the left just before you reach the end of State Highway 16. This is serious 4WD country and should only be attempted with two vehicles. There's more than a few car bodies rusting away in the sand – testaments to those who were ill-prepared.

Fishing in the lagoon at South Kaipara Head is pretty relaxing.

It's best to travel up the beach a couple of hours after high tide and return at least two hours before the next high tide. Also, if there is a big sweep on the beach, allow for this as you could get cut off earlier than expected.

For all the effort, fishing the lagoon is great fun and it's a cool place to visit. Fish with a couple of surf rods, one rigged with flashers and salted skipjack baits, the other with fresh mullet or tuatua. You will catch a real variety up here with gurnard and kahawai making up the bulk of catch, but there is always a chance of a big snapper from October through January. The most favourable winds are east or south-easterly.

Hauraki Gulf

Whangarei

Kawau Island

Little Barrier

Mokohinau Islands

Horn Rock

Great Barrier Island

Leigh

Saddle Island

Tiritiri Matangi

Whangaparaoa Peninsula

Helensville

Brazier Rock

Waiheke Island

Auckland

Mokohinau Islands

Make sure you are carrying plenty of fuel if you are travelling to the Mokohinau Islands, as the nearest refuelling spot is Port Fitzroy on Great Barrier.

This small group of rugged islands lies about 100 km northeast of Auckland and 25 km northwest of Great Barrier Island. Lying close to the edge of the continental shelf, they are an awesome spot to fish. The best way to fish them is from a launch or 6 m plus boat. The 'Mokes' do not offer any safe anchorages. If you are travelling by trailerboat the best launch sites are Mangawhai, Leigh and Omaha.

Burgess Island, the northernmost of the group and recognised by its lighthouse, is open to the public. Most of Burgess Island is scenic reserve managed by the Department of Conservation. There are no tracks or facilities and visitors are asked to be sensitive to the special conservation values of this small 50 ha island.

The remainder of the islands, including Fanal, Flax and Trig Islands, and numerous smaller rocks, are nature reserves and protected wildlife sanctuaries. Landing is not permitted without a permit.

The Mokohinau Islands offer spectacular scenery for boats exploring the surrounding waters. Formations include high cliffs and high rock spires and the diving is said to be some of the best in the country.

The Mokohinaus also produce some excellent big snapper across the edges of the reefs in depths between 45 and 50 m, such as the SW foul along from Simpson Rock. Large baits such as yellowtail, mullet and koheru work best. Trevally are sometimes caught in large numbers around Maori Rocks and Lion Rock.

In winter through to late spring, hapuku and tarakihi are quite common on the deeper reefs. Most hapuku landed are not huge fish, but they do make good eating.

The same techniques used for snapper work on hapuku. If you want to target tarakihi, try using 2/0 flasher rigs with small shellfish or squid baits.

Kingfish can be caught at the Mokes all year, but the big boys show up in late January through until April or May. Fish of 25–30 kg are not uncommon.

The area between Burgess and Maori Rocks has produced good-sized fish. To catch these large kingfish it is vital that you have a good supply of livebait: use big kahawai, slimy mackerel and koheru. Fish your baits deep by adding a 50–100 g ball sinker on top of your hook.

Perhaps the biggest attraction of the Mokohinau Islands are the big snapper that can be caught here. The whole area produces heaps of double-figure fish. Catching a monster snapper involves using the right techniques. The two favoured techniques are drift-fishing over the 40–50 m reefs with big, whole baits like live or butterflied yellowtail. This generally works well in the cooler months. Or, in summer, fish right in close to the rocks and strayline big skipjack and squid baits with absolutely no lead on the line. Casting right into the wash is often the best ploy. Use plenty of berley; kina is particularly good for this style of fishing.

Use good swivels when drift-fishing in deep water to avoid line twist.

The best baits

Live kahawai

Live koheru

Squid

Skipjack

Recommended fishing gear

10–15 kg stray lining set

100 kg trace

40 kg trace

12/0 circle hooks

8/0 suicide hooks

50–100 g ball sinkers

Good gaff

Large landing net

Sabikis

Little Barrier

Recommended fishing gear

10–15 kg straylining set
6–8 kg jig set
100 kg trace
40 kg trace
6/0 short-shank, livebait hooks
4/0 circle hooks
25 g and 50 g ball sinkers

The best baits

Fresh skipjack
Koheru

Little Barrier Island is located in the outer Hauraki Gulf some 80 km from Auckland. The same launch sites as the Mokohinau Islands are recommended. Being a round island formed by a volcano, the wind tends to sweep around the whole island, which offers little protection in strong breezes.

I have enjoyed plenty of success at Little Barrier with large snapper, kingfish and trevally, which makes it one of my favourite fishing spots. The other reason I believe I have enjoyed it so much is that I only visit the island when conditions are looking favourable, which generally involves fair weather.

While many good fish are caught at Little Barrier all year, I have found that the best time is at the beginning of winter, about when the first frost arrives. When accompanied by southeasterly winds, this is the time to target the big snapper that live around the island.

Much of the best fishing occurs in low light situations: overcast days or early mornings are favoured. Fishing in-close at depths between 3 and 20 m is where I usually fish. There are many gutters, reefs and points that fish well. As with most spots, select the areas where wind and tide are moving in the same direction. Boulder Bay on the southeastern side is a good area to fish very shallow and many big moochers have been caught here in shallow water. The submerged rocks around the Ranger's Stations

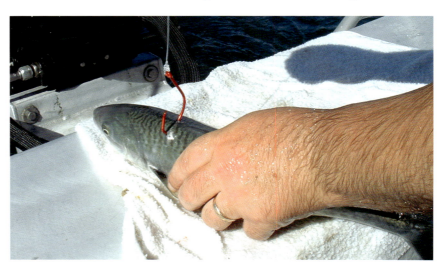

Small livebaits will be taken by kingfish, snapper and John dory at Little Barrier.

are good areas to drift with lightly weighted baits and to target kingfish with livebaits.

Moving round to the northwestern side of Little Barrier, there is a point with lots of reef. This is the best outgoing tide spot on the island. Anchor upstream of the point by about 50 m and fish back to the point with lightly weighted baits. Be sure and set up a good berley trail.

The best rising tide spot is the point that runs out a fair way from the northern end of the island. If you anchor in this area in about 20 m of water, the fish should come.

The gut between the small island and Little Barrier on the side that faces Great Barrier Island is a prime dusk spot, although bust-offs are common due to the rough terrain. Cast unweighted baits into the gap between the structures. It is important to have the current moving into the gutter so that should dictate which side you anchor.

It pays to use small, strong hooks at Little Barrier because you just don't know what you might hook next. Some of the fish, like trevally, are very delicate biters and require small baits. But it is not unusual for large fish to take the smaller baits. Putting out a live koheru, trevally or mackerel will also pay dividends, as there are lots of John dory, while kingfish and snapper also take livebaits freely.

The view of Little Barrier Island as seen from Pakiri Beach.

Horn Rock

Horn Rock is a pinnacle just over four nautical miles southeast of Little Barrier Island. This is a weather-dependent fishing spot. It is exposed to wind from all directions, so a trip should only be considered when the swell is below 1 m and light winds are forecast.

This spot is ideal for targeting big fish. Large snapper and big kingfish are in residence most of the year, with January to April being the best time.

A small rock breaks the surface; the rest of the reef lies submerged at between 10 and 20 m, dropping away to over 40 m. Divers tell me there are huge canyon-like guts that hold big crayfish and they often get buzzed by schools of kingfish.

Because there is a strong current that hits this structure, which comes out of deep water and is the only rock for miles, you can understand why it fishes so well. It's perfect habitat for prey and predator!

If kingfish are your target, slowly troll livebaits close to the exposed rock. This area is a good place to use a downrigger to get your baits deeper. Alternatively, locate the edge of the drop-off where the rock ledges fall away and drift-fish livebaits close to the bottom. Without a doubt the two best livebaits are koheru and slimy mackerel.

To target big snapper, anchor up in around 10–15 m so that you have the berley running into deeper water. Be prepared to spend a bit of time to bring the fish around and don't panic if you're not getting bites, as more often than not the first sign of fish is being connected to a monster.

Use a lightly-weighted rig with two 5/0 hooks and a whole pilchard or squid. The snapper here will take livebaits set on the bottom. It pays to fish these on heavy gear as kingies will quite often nail them.

This area is very foul so use a grapnel anchor.

Recommended fishing gear

10–15 kg straylining set
3/0 flashers
24 kg heavy game set
24 kg trace
100 kg trace
9/0 short-shank livebait hooks
5/0 suicide hooks
25 g ball sinkers

The best baits

Live koheru
Live slimy mackerel
Pilchard
Squid

Downriggers are great for controlled-depth fishing with livebaits and lures.

Great Barrier Island

How do you describe a spot that, from a fisherman's and most other people's perspective, has got so much going for it? It has excellent fishing, from rock, boat or beach, unrivalled scenery, a host of outdoor activities, and if you desire serene isolation, Great Barrier Island has the kind of ruggedness that is typically New Zealand.

Accessible by sea or air, Great Barrier Island, also known as Aotea, has a permanent population of around 1300. It lies only two hours from Auckland by ferry and is a quick 30-minute plane trip.

'The Barrier,' as it is commonly known, because it is the barrier that protects the Hauraki Gulf from the Pacific swell, is a fantastic place to explore and offers many safe anchorages and places to stay for all types of boats.

For the land-based angler there are spots aplenty. Cape Barrier Rocks, which are at the southern end of the island, is popular with hardcore land-based game fishermen who use 4 m inflatable boats to access the ledges.

The main targets are the big snapper and kingfish that hunt in the shallows. Livebaiting with 2 kg kahawai suspended under inflated party balloons attached to the swivel with cotton or dental floss is the way to attract the big kingfish.

Large baits of skipjack and mullet cast into the kelp will entice the kelpie snapper. Frequently snapper will come right up to the rocks if a good berley trail is set up.

Heading north from Cape Barrier is an island. I call it 'Rabbit Island', but don't quote me on its name. I have fond memories of the ledge at the front of the island. While fishing one day I caught and released six snapper over 9 kg, in six casts! A good friend of mine, and a guy who showed me more than one spot in this book, Richard Baker, landed a 42 kg kingie off the ledge and topped it off with 9 kg snapper!

The most important factor for this spot is current. If the current is not running, the fishing is never as good. So, if you intend to try it, look for the biggest tides possible. While there are many other good rock spots, evidenced by the number of heli-fishing trips that come to the Barrier, the

There are several options for accommodation – lodges, home stays, cottages or camping. Supplies are available on the island and some shops have Eftpos, but there are no banking facilities.

You can get to the island by sea or air, and, once there, transport and tours include taxis, rental cars, mountain bikes, kayak tours and tour operators.

Camping grounds have basic facilities like long-drop toilets and cold water, and they cost around $6 a night. There are DOC camping grounds in all the popular places on the island, as well as commercial camping grounds, which are also quite cheap, though you might pay a little more for extra facilities.

A selection of tuna lures.

Recommended fishing gear

10–15 kg boat set

8–10 kg jig set

4/0 flasher rigs

150 g jigs

24 kg trace

100 kg trace

8/0 suicide hooks

10/0 livebait hooks

6–8 oz teardrop sinkers

The best baits

Pilchard

Live kahawai

Piper

Skipjack

Squid

other spot worth fishing is the beach at Okiwi, on the eastern side of the island. Catching kahawai and trevally in the surf here is just plain good fun and it's a great place to take the family fishing.

Boat fishing offers even more opportunities than shore fishing. Inshore, small boats and kayaks can spend days fishing the many sheltered bays and points. In the deeper water off the east coast during summer, yellowfin tuna and marlin migrate and can be caught by trolling game lures in 100–150 m of water.

For the snapper fisherman, early November is when the snapper get ready to spawn off the west coast and vast schools can be found in 40 m of water a few kilometres off the island. They are often accompanied by huge work-ups with gannets, dolphins and whales. These snapper are normally ravenous and once located will take baits and jigs with gusto.

Moving inshore on the west coast there are two prime spots: a group of islands – the Broken Islands – located in the middle of Barrier and a large reef at the entrance to Tryphena Harbour. Both of these spots offer great fishing for a wide variety of species.

At the northern end of Great Barrier is a point called Miners Head. Directly out from here is Miners Reef. Anchoring near the reef in 20–40 m will produce snapper, tarakihi, kingfish and the odd hapuku at times.

Arid Island, also known as Rakitu, lies off the eastern side of the Barrier, and when conditions allow, it is well worth a visit. Try to anchor on one of the many pinnacles near the island – you will be treated to a wide variety of fish: snapper, trevally and porae. Tarakihi and hapuku can be caught once the depth is over 50 m. Baited flasher rigs are the best approach to catching fish at Arid.

Lots of good ledges can be accessed in a small boat.

Kawau Island

Kawau is the first of the inner Hauraki Gulf Islands, situated to the north of Auckland. Fishing around the island can be challenging at times; during late winter and early spring the snapper definitely move around a lot and can be hard to find. From late spring onwards, the fishing becomes much more predictable and the fish easier to catch.

After the major runs of school snapper, the fish tend to move out to the eastern side of the island, where they take up residence on two major reef complexes.

Nelson Reef is the closest to Kawau and easy to find, as it is normally dotted with plenty of crayfish pots. The best way to fish Nelson Reef is to anchor up on top of the reef where there is some sign of fish. Obviously, you need a sounder to do this.

Alternatively, fish off the back of the reef where it drops off onto the sand. Use a running rig with a sinker that suits the current, which can really rip at times. Weigh your berley down and set it on the bottom to ensure it is effective.

Flat Rock is marked by a beacon that sometimes can be mistaken for a sailboat on the horizon. You can catch fish on Flat Rock itself, but the best spots lie about kilometre further out where there is a group of three submerged reefs. Anchoring on any one of these bumps and straylining

Kawau is a horseshoe-shaped island with a host of sheltered bays and anchorages. It is easily accessed by small craft that can launch at any number of sites on the mainland. Sandspit and Snells Beach are the most popular.

The island is serviced by a ferry that leaves from Sandspit and a water taxi service also operates in the area. A shop with basic provisions and a fuelling service are located in Bon Accord Harbour.

A piper rigged for casting and trolling.

The best baits

Mackerel fillet
Live kahawai
Live koheru
Fresh piper
Mullet

Recommended fishing gear

6–8 kg straylining set
15 kg heavy livebait rig
100 kg trace
40 kg trace
9/0 short-shank livebait hooks
6/0 suicide hooks
50 g ball sinkers

with next to no weight can produce very big snapper from January to April. One trick here is to use hard baits like fillets of yellowtail and kahawai, because maomao and other reef fish demolish softer baits like pilchards.

Over summer there are generally a few nice kingfish hanging around this area, so it is always worth putting out a livebait while you are snapper fishing.

On the northern end of Kawau Island is a small exposed reef called 'Fairchild'. Fairchild does produce a few snapper and kingfish, but if you continue heading across the North Channel towards Tawharanui Peninsula you will find Maori Rock. This is a spot where the kingfish bite really well. Casting piper and skipping them back across the surface with a rapid retrieve or livebaiting with koheru and small kahawai will invoke plenty of strikes. Snapper fishing at Maori Rock can be good if the tide is going out at dawn or dusk. Anchor 80 m up-current and fish back onto the reef.

At the end of Tawharanui there is a little bay just before you reach Takatu Point. If you're quiet and get in really close where you can see the bottom and berley up heaps, this bay will produce lots of good trevally and snapper. Use small baits and keep the noise down.

Right on the end of Takatu Point is another good area to target kingfish. From what I have been told, kingfish go here because cleaner fish living in the area remove parasites from the kingfish's bodies. True or not, the kingies are definitely there. Slowly troll with livebait back and forth around the point.

Scallops are plentiful around Kawau Island.

Saddle Island

The small island located just off the mouth of Mahurangi Harbour may seem a little innocuous, but Saddle Island is a kingfish hotspot. From late December each year large schools of kingfish take up residence near this island, feeding on the baitfish that are pushed out of Mahurangi.

A good supply of bait is very important for success. Bait-size kahawai can be caught by trolling small silver lures around the mouth of the harbour, or by fishing small baits of unweighted pilchard in a berley trail up the harbour around the oyster farm. Piper can be attracted in the shallow bays with bread crumbs and caught by fishing with size 16 trout hooks baited with small bits of squid suspended under a float.

At Saddle Island the best spot is the broken reef at the northern tip. Troll livebaits and piper as slowly as possible about 5 m from the reef. The fish bite on both the rising and falling tide with tides over 3 m providing better current.

Saddle Island is close to shore, making it an ideal location for small boats and kayaks to fish. It can be accessed from the Mahurangi or Wenderholm boat ramps, but these ramps are unworkable at half-tide or less.

Having the gear to catch livebait is half the battle when chasing kingfish.

The kingies usually attack in packs and multiple hook-ups are common around the point. Be prepared and lead the kingfish away from the reef to avoid being broken off on the reef.

Recommended fishing gear

10–15kg livebaiting set

3 kg spin set

7 g jigs

60 kg trace

6/0 livebait hooks

10/0 livebait hooks

Size 16 trout hooks

Small bubble floats

Best baits

Live kahawai

Piper

I remember fishing here one day. It was quite foggy and calm. I launched at Wenderholm and found the kahawai working right on the hotspot. I caught bait at will and each time I put one out it was attacked by a pack of kingies almost instantly. That morning I caught and released three fish of round 25 kg in about two hours.

Saddle Island sits at the entrance to Mahurangi Harbour.

The boat ramp at Wenderholm.

Brazier Rock

Brazier Rock is also known as the Wenderholm Reef. Turn right into Wenderholm Regional Park just past Waiwera thermal pools, about an hour north of Auckland off State Highway 1.

Launching for boats up to 6 m is good two hours each side of the high tide. The ramp is near the mouth of the Puhoi River and the narrow channels get a little shallow at low tide. The concrete ramp has very little fall.

Brazier Rock is easy to see from shore, as it is exposed and has a marker on it. The area does not receive too much attention from anglers, which is probably why it is one of the more consistent snapper spots year round.

The tricks to catching fish here are fairly straightforward. Anchor on one of the submerged bits of reef off the back of the main rock. The depth varies from 6 to 8 m. Make sure you have a constant berley trail and occasionally toss in a few cubes of pilchard. Use 4–6 kg tackle with small hooks and light sinkers.

The fish will bite on both sides of the tide and tend to get more active in the late afternoon. Fish with two rods. Set the second rod in the holder with a larger bait like a fillet of yellowtail as you do get fish over 4 kg here pretty regularly.

The gates to the park open about 7 am and shut at about 8 pm in summer.

Recommended fishing gear

4–6 kg light outfit
15 kg trace
4/0 recurve hooks

Best baits

Pilchard
Piper
Squid
Yellowtail fillets

John Eichelsheim with a pan-sized snapper caught at Brazier Rock.

Tiritiri Matangi

Situated 4 km seawards from the tip of Whangaparaoa Peninsula, about 25 km north of Auckland, Tiri is home to the oldest lighthouse in the Hauraki Gulf. It was erected in 1864 and subsequently upgraded 100 years later with a beacon fifty times more powerful than the old light, extending its beam nearly 50 km, making it the brightest in the Southern Hemisphere.

The best launching site for all boats is at the Gulf Harbour boat ramp at the end of Whangaparaoa Peninsula, but it is exposed to wind from the south and west.

Best baits

Pilchard
Live mackerel
Squid

Recommended fishing gear

3/0 flasher rigs
20 kg trace
50 kg trace
10/0 livebaiting hooks
6/0 suicide hooks
90 g jigs
Bibbed minnows

The channel you cross from Whangaparaoa on the way to Tiri can become very rough when wind opposes tide, so keep an eye on the weather.

Fishing at the southern end of the Tiri Channel can be very good from October through to early January when the major snapper schooling runs take place. Use either a dropper rig or a running rig baited with pilchard or squid.

The current rips strongly here, so don't be afraid of using a bit of lead to hold the bottom. The fish bite on the running tide and tend to be a fairly uniform size of 1.5–2 kg. When they are on, limit bags can be caught very quickly.

Moving up to the northwestern tip of the island you will see marked on the hydrographic chart or your GPS a submerged rock known as Boland's Rock. This is an interesting spot to fish, as one of the keys to success is the use of very long traces, up to 3 m, with a running rig. For some reason this works very well and many good hauls of snapper have been caught using this technique. Fishing fires best here on an early morning incoming tide.

Moving around to the eastern side of Tiri, many anglers like to fish right under the lighthouse and I'm sure they do well. If you move off the island and fish a little south of the channel between Tiri and Shearer Rock, you will find quite a bit of foul bottom. This is one of the areas that produces many double-figure snapper. The trick here is using whole yellowtail for bait, either live or dead.

A rather interesting quirk of Tiri is that many big snapper get caught on bibbed minnows aimed at kingfish. On more than one occasion I have caught 8 kg plus snapper while trolling for kingfish and I have spoken to other anglers who have had similar experiences. This may be due to where the snapper feed on the edge of the drop-offs and around sub-surface structure.

There is a marker buoy showing the position of Shearer Reef, which is not to be confused with Shearer Rock, about a kilometre off the southeastern side of the island. The marker buoy usually has a resident school of kingfish that can provide good sport on poppers cast to and retrieved quickly away from the buoy. Most of these kingies are fairly small, but don't be surprised if you see the odd big one.

Shearer Reef runs north of the marker and fishes very well for snapper when you have an outgoing tide and light winds from the west. Again, this is a spot where double-figure fish are common – we have had them taking baits barely a foot from the surface at the back of the boat. Stealth and a good berley trail are vital.

It's not uncommon to see large work-ups of terns and gannets off Tiri, especially when pilchards and anchovies are schooling in December through to February. It is always worth travelling out to see if the fish are with the work-ups. Use 90 g jigs or drift through the work-ups with baited flasher rigs for fast and furious action; sometimes you will find snapper, kingfish, trevally, kahawai and John dory. At other times these work-ups will be barren of fish.

Fishing livebaits deep works well at Tiri.

Whangaparaoa Peninsula

The Peninsula juts out into the Hauraki Gulf and offers shelter on its opposing shores from northerly and southerly winds, and the tip offers a lee shore in a southwesterly.

You cannot anchor or fish off the very tip of Whangaparaoa Peninsula at certain times because the Army has a training firing range at the end of the peninsula. Also, there are underwater cables clearly marked. Small craft can be launched easily at Army Bay; larger boats should launch at Gulf Harbour.

Recommended fishing gear

8 kg strayline set
6 kg jig set
24 kg trace
15 kg trace
2/0 flasher rigs
4/0 suicide hooks
60 g jigs

Best baits

Fresh slimy mackerel
Pilchard
Squid
Salted bonito

This is one of the nice things about the peninsula: it can be fished in most winds except a strong easterly. Whangaparaoa is also very popular with small boat and kayak anglers.

The preferred side to fish is the northern side from Army Bay up to the tip. The reason for this is masses of shallow reef and weed that hold good numbers of fish most of the year. The premium time to fish the Army Bay Reef is when the large slimy mackerel turn up. This is usually about October or November. These mackerel get up to 2 kg in weight and bite on small flashers and baits at dawn and dusk. Not only are they great sport, fighting like a kahawai on speed, they also are great to eat. And, used fresh, they are excellent bait.

Looking at your chart you will notice a big 'brick' straight out from Army Bay. This is Wellington Reef, a spot that fishes well on a rising tide at change of light. Use the same techniques as for Army Bay – and if you catch livebait put one out because John dory and kingfish are frequent visitors to this rock.

Jig-fishing is pretty good when you move further out into the bay. There is no specific spot; look for working birds and drop you jigs under them.

If you want to catch a quick feed of fish, drift half a kilometre off the back of Orewa Beach with small flashers baited with salted bonito or pilchard. Gurnard can be found on the sand here at most times.

On the southern side of the Whangaparaoa Peninsula is the Oakura River. Fishing the shallow flats in 2–3 m of water out from the mouth can produce some surprisingly large snapper and trevally. Like most shallow water spots, keeping boat noise down and using a good berley trail at change of light is how to get the fish going here. The best fishing seems to be from I March through till May. You can launch a boat in the river, but it is extremely tidal and can be hard work. Take care not to stray into the adjacent Long Bay Marine Reserve.

A couple of prime snapper caught out of my kayak while fishing at Army Bay.

Waiheke Island

The second-largest island in the Hauraki Gulf, and the most developed, Waiheke Island is where the bulk of fishing is done by Aucklanders, and despite the pressure, it still produces excellent results.

Located a short trip from Half Moon Bay Marina in East Auckland, or any of a dozen other boat ramps in the Auckland region, Waiheke is a fisherman's dream. It offers seas that are protected from all prevailing conditions, miles of coastline to explore, safe anchorages and a wide variety of fishing.

The first spot is actually not on Waiheke but off Pakatoa Island, which is located at the end of the Waiheke Channel at the southern end of the island. There is a long reef that runs out from Pakatoa towards the bottom end of Waiheke. The depth range is from 5 to 14 m. Slow-trolling live kahawai along the contour of the reef will trigger strike after strike from hungry kingfish during the season that runs from November to May. The kingies range in size from 10 to 20 kg. Fishing is best on the rising tide and the start of the outgoing.

To catch livebaits use a paravane and simple silver spoon. Troll along the edge of the Waiheke Channel where large schools of kahawai are often bubbling on the surface.

Waiheke is a day trip for most powerboats and has plenty of safe anchorages. Passenger ferries leave from downtown Auckland and vehicle ferries from Half Moon Bay Marina. A full range of services is available on Waiheke but accommodation should be pre-booked at all times.

Boiling kahawai is a sight that gets the blood fizzing.

Looking out to sea there is a pyramid-shaped rock called Tarakihi Island, also known as Shag Rock by fishermen for reasons that are obvious when you see the number of shags that live there. This spot also produces superb kingie fishing, but mainly on the outgoing tide. Use the same techniques as for Pakatoa in about 9 m of water off the western side of the island. Pack-attacks of kingfish are a common sight and fish up to 40 kg have been caught here, though the average would be 15 kg.

An angler gets his arms stretched at Shag Rock.

A good trick for this spot if the fishing is quiet or you don't have livebait is to use a flutter bait. This is a kahawai that has been butterflied and rigged with a 50 g sinker mounted on top of a 10/0 livebait hook. Set this bait about a metre from the bottom and let the boat's action make it flutter.

Kingfish normally turn their noses up at dead baits unless they are feeding hard-out, but this rig works really well even when the fishing is tough.

For anglers seeking snapper, the area at the bottom end of Waiheke from Shag Rock across to Kauri Point and out into the Hauraki Gulf and Firth of Thames is a major snapper congregation area from late October through to early December. These massive schools only last for a short time and then break up in smaller groups in specific spots.

The area of foul that runs off Kauri Point and lies in water 6 to 20 m deep is very productive when the tide run is strong. This spot fishes best on the incoming tide when the wind is in the northwest and on the outgoing tide when the wind is southeast or southwest. A standard running rig and mullet bait is the top rig here and put your berley on the bottom.

In winter, fish the shallow parts of the reef with strayline rigs as there are always resident snapper in the cooler months.

In spring there is a big run of John dory in the whole bottom end of the Waiheke area, so it is worth drifting along the edges of the drop-offs and channels jigging with 90 to 150 g chrome jigs or fishing a live yellowtail on the bottom when you are snapper fishing.

Heading north from Kauri Point past Hooks Bay, you will see Thumb Point. While Thumb Point is a recognised spot, the next point north has proved far more productive for me. This spot fishes well all year round for school fish. During winter you tend to catch fewer fish, but the fish are better quality.

This spot only fires on the rising tide and requires accurate anchoring because baits must be fished where the bottom falls away. If you've set the anchor properly, the boat will end up directly off the point with the stern pointing straight at Thumb Point. A constant stream of berley will bring the fish to the area.

Baits should be cast well back from the boat and allowed to sink as naturally as possible. Large juicy pieces of fresh skipjack work well in winter and pilchards and squid are better in summer.

On the seaward side of Thumb Point is a large rock covered in guano (bird droppings). This is Gannet Rock, home to a large gannet colony, and if approached from down wind on a hot day, it is a very smelly place.

Recommended fishing gear

10–15 kg boat set
6–8 kg jig set
4/0 flasher rigs
90 g jigs
24 kg trace
100 kg trace
4/0 suicide hooks
10/0 livebait hooks
Paravane
Silver kahawai lures

Best baits

Pilchard
Live kahawai
Piper
Skipjack
Squid

Success at Gannet Rock.

A beaten kingfish lies beside the boat prior to release.

Large schools of maomao and baitfish live around Gannet Rock and there are plenty of mussels around the low water mark. I'm not sure of the eating quality of these mussels due to all the bird 'nutrients' in the water, but they are a source of food for the fish.

Gannet Rock does produce its share of big snapper – when it's on, it fires like nothing else. Casting large, unweighted baits in the gap between the rocks on the seaward side of the island is one way to get strikes or try anchoring on the reef just on the inside tip of the island and about 300 m to the north. A sounder will get you right on it. Dragging livebaits around the island and onto the surrounding reef structure will produce good action from kingfish in summer.

D'Urville Rock is an isolated rock about 3 km north of Gannet Rock that just breaks the surface. It has a marker showing its whereabouts. The underwater structure is rather like an inverted mushroom, with the reef spreading out for a considerable distance like an upside-down mushroom's cap and part of it coming up as a stalk where it breaks the surface. Plenty of weed and shelter attract baitfish, squid and predators. On calm winter days in June-August D'Urville can really turn it on.

Positioning on this spot is fairly general. The best areas are well off the marker, where the reef drops away onto the sand. Pick the side that will let your berley travel over the reef with the tide and wind movement. The bites can be pretty random here as the fish are attracted from quite a distance, so a good way to fill in time is to catch yellowtail on sabikis and use them as livebait for John dory, which are prolific on this structure.

Moving straight inshore from D'Urville, the point on the northern entrance to Onetangi Bay is a bit of a gem. Thompsons Point is one of those spots that is easy to drive past. Anchor within 100 m, straight off the point. Berley from the surface and rig up with light tackle, 4/0 hooks and up to 25–50 g sinkers if necessary. Cast half-pilchards or cut baits of bonito down the berley trail.

Fishing here one day during a fishing competition, we caught nothing for the first couple of hours. After a while I took my sinker off and started casting my bonito baits a bit further than the other guys on the boat. As my baits were sinking they started getting slammed by good snapper. My fishing buddies followed suit and were soon into the fish. At the weigh-in we ended up in the money with fourth-heaviest snapper, first-, second- and third-heaviest kahawai and first- and second-heaviest John dory. We were well-pleased with this result at Thompsons Point and it shows a little change in tactics, like fishing without a sinker or putting livebait down, can radically change your fortunes.

Waitemata Harbour

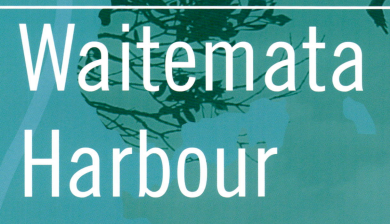

North Shore

Massey

Auckland

Inner Harbour

East Coast Bays

Rangitoto Island

Outer Harbour

The Noises and Ahaaha Rocks

Browns Island

Waitemata Harbour and East Coast Bays

The East Coast Bays of Auckland's North Shore are well serviced with boat ramps for smaller craft. Takapuna can handle boats up to 7 m. Takapuna is not good in winds from the north and east. From Auckland, the best public ramps are at Westhaven and the Akarana Yacht Club. These ramps are all-weather, all-tide ramps for all vessels. Parking fees apply.

Protected by the surrounding islands and the mainland, the Waitemata Harbour is serviced by three main channels. The Rangitoto Channel leads north and is used as the main shipping channel in and out of the harbour, the Motuihe Channel runs east and Tamaki Strait lies to the southeast.

When the spring snapper runs start, usually in October or November, snapper use the channels as corridors and can be caught easily by fishing on the edge of the channels with running rigs and ledger rigs. The male fish run first then the larger females show up two to three weeks later.

As with all fishing you have to move around to find the fish as they will hold in different positions depending on the wind and the tide. While this annual run of fish is the only fishing a lot of anglers know, many persevere fishing the channels long after the runs have slowed down and the fish have moved to inshore reefs and the inner harbour.

Having a basic understanding of where the fish move and their habits in the Waitemata can make it easier to target them. Snapper, after they have run, will remain in areas that offer shelter and food. Rarely will you find them in areas where the bottom is flat and lifeless, unless an

The Rangitoto Lighthouse.

Fishing with light tackle pays dividends in the Waitemata Harbour.

abundant food source is present, like, for example, when predators such as kahawai and kingfish ambush a school of baitfish. Then the snapper will forage on the scraps.

In general the best places to hunt for snapper are reefs and foul territory that are close to food. Snapper move a short distance away from cover at dawn and dusk to feed.

Auckland's North Shore is characterised by a series of sandy bays broken up by a volcanic rocky foreshore with plenty of exposed and submerged reefs. Some of it is very close to the edge of the Rangitoto Channel.

Browns Bay, Castor Bay, Takapuna Reef, Thorns Bay and right down to Narrowneck Beach are superb spots a few hundred metres offshore, making them ideal for small tinnies and kayaks.

The fishing approach and techniques used for this area are all the same, hence grouping them as one area. Fish can be caught all year with February through to late May being the most consistent period. If the wind is from the southwest, both incoming and outgoing tides will fish well. In a northerly only the incoming tide works and southeast is the worst wind. The fish bite for longer periods in the early morning and late afternoon, but they really shut down during the period of the full moon.

Fishing with light tackle (no heavier than 6–8 kg line), using 2 m rods with a whippy tip action and developing a deft feel for light bites are definite advantages in these shallow-water spots that are rarely deeper than 8 m. The best approach is to anchor up on or around the area you wish to fish, allowing for the direction of the tide so that your berley will pull fish off the reef. Use a combination of ground berley and chopped up cubes of pilchard.

Recommended fishing gear

6–8 kg casting set
4/0 flasher rigs
60 g jigs
15 kg trace
4/0 suicide hooks
5/0 circle hooks

Best baits

Pilchard
Piper
Skipjack
Squid
Mullet gut
Mullet

Fish with a couple of rods; cast one well back from the boat with a whole bait like piper or squid and fish the other closer in the berley trail with a small cube of pilchard or strip of mullet. Bites can be quite tentative and fishing with reels in free spool and letting fish run off with the bait before striking or slowly lifting the rod as soon as weight comes on are two techniques that make the difference between solid hook-ups and bare hooks.

Many anglers complain about the number of small fish cleaning up their bait, and while a lot of juvenile fish are present, the problem can stem from not maintaining contact with baits and poor strike timing.

Kingfish, bronze whaler sharks and John dory also patrol the outer edges of the East Coast Bays and on days when bird or kahawai activity is sighted, jigging along the edge of the reefs with 60 g lures will produce good mixed bags. Casting poppers at the kingfish that hang around the many structures and channel markers can also produce good action.

Inside Bean Rock, the large house-like structure in the middle of the Waitemata Harbour and out from Mission Bay, Kohimarama and Ladies Bay, lies another group of shallow reefs, which are clearly indicated by navigation poles. The water around these reefs is only a few metres deep. During the day they are normally devoid of any major fish, but fishing them in darkness just before dawn will turn up amazing fishing.

These spots are best approached in small boats and kayaks. A light northerly and high tide at around 9 am are the conditions to look for from February to April.

On many mornings I have fished here with friends and joked about "what the rich people were doing" as we watched Auckland commuters battling their way to work through the traffic, then looked at the bunch of 4 kg snapper we had caught. These spots will turn up big fish as well – fish over 6 kg are fairly common.

Fishing with multiple rods will increase your chances of getting fish.

Rangitoto Island 🎣

The large volcanic cone of Rangitoto Island is one of the focal points of the Waitemata Harbour. The hardened lava rocks spill into the water all around the island and form many reefs and points. Rangitoto Island is covered in a blanket of trees and when cloud surrounds the cone, it can look quite primeval.

The Rangitoto Lighthouse is situated at the entrance of the northern end of Rangitoto Channel and marks a large reef complex. Fishing around the edge of this reef system and just off the lighthouse produces nice snapper and kingfish from December to May.

Moving just around the lighthouse to the lava flows on the northeastern side of the island, strayline fishing in the latter part of summer and early autumn can be spectacular. Anchor off one of the many points in 10–15 m of water and fish with lightly weighted pilchard baits.

During winter land-based fishers and anglers fishing out of small boats fish right off the rocks in this area of the lava flows, and although fishing can be slow, the rewards are well worth it with snapper in excess of 10 kg and large trevally being caught.

Anchoring in Rangitoto Channel between the channel markers is prohibited.

Recommended fishing gear
6–8 kg casting set
10 kg boat set
15 kg trace
4/0 suicide hooks
5/0 circle hooks
25–200 g sinkers

Best baits
Pilchard
Squid
Mullet
Piper

A bunch of happy anglers with the results of a dusk charter to Rangitoto Island.

The reefs around Rangitoto are very productive in May.

The area inside number two channel marker down to the barges is very popular with charter boats during summer. Many reefs and channel edges make the ideal environment for snapper to hole up. Patches of fish can be found here at most times. A running tide is preferred and time spent locating fish schools on the sounder will pay dividends.

In the cooler months snapper can be targeted by straylining the inner reefs and headlands with light tackle and plenty of berley. Combining wind and tide from the same direction with dawn and dusk fishing will provide the best results.

Inner Harbour

Travel under the Auckland Harbour Bridge to the area known as the Inner Harbour, and the terrain changes once again, with shallow, small arterial channels running in all directions; deep holes straight off sandstone cliffs and vast areas of shallow, flat banks.

Launching sites are located at Westpark Marina in West Auckland, Island Bay, Birkenhead Point and Bayswater on the North Shore or Westhaven, OBC and Akarana on the city side. Boat traffic can put the fish off here. Avoid anchoring in the channels.

Many people drive straight past great fishing in the inner harbour.

One large reef complex runs out from Point Chevalier to form Meola Reef in the centre of the Inner Harbour. Meola Reef fishes much the same as the reefs already mentioned in this chapter and using the same tactics will produce results.

Moving down the main channel on the northern side of the harbour a series of deep holes up to 40 m deep have been formed by the strong tidal flow hitting the sandstone cliffs. Kauri Point is the most prominent of these holes and is marked on hydrographic charts. Snapper start to move into the Inner Harbour in January. At this time fish can be caught by fishing into the Kauri Point hole. Use a ledger rig with plenty of lead to hold the bottom. Berley must be heavily weighted and set on the bottom to have any effect.

The running tide is best for the Kauri Point hole, and keep baits small, as sharks and rays can be a problem. Anchoring can be tricky here

Recommended fishing gear

8 kg boat set

4–6 kg casting set

4/0 flasher rigs

60 g jigs

15 kg trace

4/0 suicide hooks

5/0 circle hooks

6–12 oz teardrop sinkers

Best baits

Pilchard

Squid

Mullet

because of the bottom structure and current. You will need a good anchor and plenty of chain to get a good hold, otherwise you will drag all day.

For the better part of summer and autumn, when the snapper have entered the inner harbour, good fish can be caught by fishing the edge of the shallow channels and any small depressions where the water depth increases on the rising tide. The increase may only be from 2 m to 4 m.

As the snapper work up on the banks they feed on the vast shellfish beds. This fishing is extremely tide critical and requires a high degree of stealth. If you locate a hole or small side channel that is holding fish you will be able to catch fish from it all summer when the tides are early morning or late afternoon.

Fishing from my kayak, I have regularly caught fish to 4 kg on the edge of the channel on the third red marker out from Westpark Marina. They've been in the frying pan for breakfast by 9 am that morning.

A couple of inner harbour snapper caught out of the kayak.

Browns Island

At mouth of the Tamaki River and the northern end of Tamaki Strait and Motuihe Channel, Browns Island offers a couple of fishing options.

The reef that is clearly marked on the side of the island that faces the Tamaki River is a top early morning and dusk spot. Cast unweighted baits close to the reef and berley with a steady stream of pilchard cubes.

This is one of those spots that produces surprisingly large snapper, especially considering it is so close to the Half Moon Bay Marina, and it fishes well in most winds and tides.

On the northern side of the island is a single reef marker and it is always worth dropping a small kahawai livebait in here as kingfish are present in good numbers over summer.

Unlike most fishing spots, lots of noise and plenty of propeller wash seems to draw the inquisitive kingies to livebaits.

Boat traffic can be a problem here on busy weekends and public holidays.

Recommended fishing gear
6–8 kg casting set
10 kg livebait set
15 kg trace
40 kg trace
4/0 suicide hooks
6/0 livebait hooks

Best baits
Pilchard
Small, live kahawai
Trevally cut baits

The Browns Island beacon is a good spot to livebait for kingfish.

Outer Harbour

Motutapu Island and neighbouring Rakino Island, along with Motuihe Island, offer several excellent areas to fish with both close-in straylining and channel fishing possible.

Conditions, terrain and techniques are the same as for Rangitoto Island and require little further information other than reinforcing the point of keeping wind and tide in the same direction.

More importantly, a seasonal migration of baitfish enters the area surrounded by this group of islands around February. The baitfish are anchovies and can be seen in massive balls in the water, often accompanied by large schools of feeding kahawai, kingfish and birds.

The best technique for fishing these work-ups is to drift-fish and jig with 40 to 90 g jigs. Snapper and trevally lie under these melées and will take jigs fished on the bottom and yo-yoed by rising and lowering the rod tip.

A useful piece of kit when jigging in this situation is a small sea anchor or drogue. Deployed when you reach a spot, it will slow down drift speed in windy conditions, allowing jigs more time in the strike zone. Jigs need to be fished vertically for best results; get too much angle away from the boat and fish won't strike.

Boat traffic can be a problem here on busy weekends and public holidays.

Recommended fishing gear

6–8 kg jig set
40–90 g jigs (rigged with single hooks)
4/0 flasher rigs
Small sea anchor

Best baits

Pilchard
Anchovy

You know the fish are "on" when the boats line up across the Motuihe Channel.

The Noises and Ahaaha Rocks

Three small islands and lots of semi-submerged reefs make up The Noises and Ahaaha Rocks. This area divides the outer areas of the Waitemata Harbour and the Hauraki Gulf. The best route to reach them is north via the Motuihe Channel. Fishing in this region is fairly productive over summer with plenty of snapper, kingfish and John dory in residence. Fishing close to the drop-offs and shallow reefs will be rewarded.

The best time to fish here is when the big snapper move in to the outer reefs prior to spawning. This situation only happens for a few weeks each year – any time from August through to November. The best conditions are just after a decent blow when the water is still disturbed and coloured with plenty of food dislodged from the rocks.

The spots to look for are where the prevailing wind will allow the stern of the boat to face into a bay or break in the reef or island where the fish will be foraging. At this time and place, big, unweighted baits rigged with big 7/0–9/0 hooks is the way to go. Whole pilchards and squid or large pieces of skipjack cast into the shallow water will attract attention from the snapper in the area. Patience and a good berley made up of mussels and kina will help your chances.

Take care when navigating this area, as many of the reefs are just submerged at high tide.

Recommended fishing gear

10–15 kg strayline set
7/0–9/0 suicide hooks
30 kg trace
Mussel and kina berley

Best baits

Pilchard
Squid
Skipjack

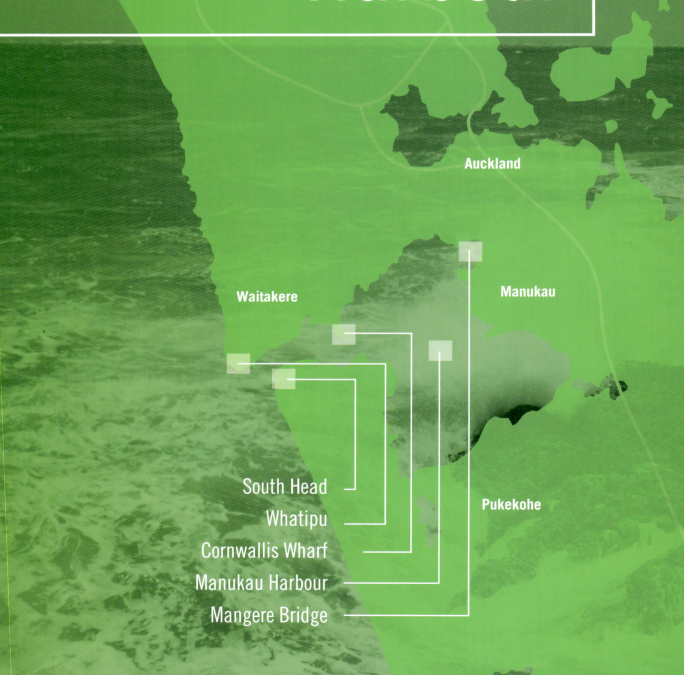

Manukau
Harbour

Auckland

Waitakere

Manukau

Pukekohe

South Head

Whatipu

Cornwallis Wharf

Manukau Harbour

Mangere Bridge

Manukau Harbour

Vastly different from the Waitemata, the Manukau Harbour at first glance appears to be a shallow, muddy-looking harbour with little to offer anglers. This appearance is totally deceiving; the Manukau looks muddy due to the vast volumes of water that come in and out every six hours across the narrow entrance at the heads. The shallow banks are rich in nutrients and offer a wealth of fishing opportunities and vast beds of shellfish.

The Manukau Harbour is full of mud banks and channels. A good chart is essential.

Lying to the west of Auckland, the Manukau can get very choppy due to its shallow nature and strong currents, but as it's almost circular, you can always find a sheltered spot to fish. Boats can be launched at ramps dotted all the way around the harbour, but many are not so good at low tide.

The Manukau offers many options for shore-based fishermen, starting with fairly easy to access spots right through to places that require a fair degree of fitness to get to.

Mangere Bridge

Little if any fishing is done above the Mangere Bridge, but fishing off the old Mangere Bridge can provide good sport on kahawai. Fish with a stout surf rod rigged with a ledger rig and mullet baits, or simply use a small chrome lure on the outgoing tide and the current will give the lure action.

Cornwallis Wharf

Driving west out through Titirangi, the many small, shallow bays offer good flounder spearing at night during December, January and February.

Cornwallis Wharf is signposted about 20 km past Titirangi. Here boats can be launched at high tide with 4WD vehicles.

Cornwallis Wharf is a great spot to introduce kids to fishing, as the area is always alive with sprats and piper. Set the kids up with light spinning rods rigged with a small, light float and size 16 trout hooks baited with dough made from flour and water or a string of sabikis baited with small flakes of mullet flesh.

For parents it's also worth casting a surf rod out as kahawai and gurnard are fairly common straight off the end of the wharf. The occasional kingfish is also caught off Cornwallis Wharf by more adventurous anglers who put out livebaits.

Whatipu

Further on from Cornwallis, as you pass Little Huia, you will have to drive 7 km on a very narrow, winding gravel road. This leads to Whatipu on the north head of the Manukau Harbour. From Whatipu carpark you will have to walk for 15 minutes to get to the beach and rocks.

Paratutai Island at the Manukau Heads.

Whatipu epitomises all that is good and bad about the west coast. It can be spectacular and offer great fishing, as it is just inside the Manukau Bar. On the other hand, it can be windy, rough and dangerous with surging tidal currents racing along at 5 to 6 knots. Whatipu is definitely not a swimming beach.

Kahawai are the most common catch and are present all year. In winter and spring good runs of trevally are encountered off the rocks and beach. Low tide and the last two hours of the outgoing tide and start of the incoming tide are the best times to fish because the swell is greatly reduced when the water level drops as it is stopped by the bar.

The best surfcasting area on the beach is from the north of Nine Pin Rock up to the lagoon. Trevally, gurnard and kahawai are caught consistently, with snapper visiting in spring and summer.

The larger island to the left of the track when you hit the beach is

Paratutai. You can get onto Paratutai at low tide, but beware – you can get cut off at high tide and once you go past the remains of the old wharf, it can be a very dangerous place.

The bottom here is full of snags, so expect to lose a fair bit of gear. The most popular technique is to fish small livebaits like sprats and yellowtail suspended under a plastic float or piece of polystyrene to catch kahawai and kingfish.

When the mullet spawn around Whatipu from November to February, a good run of kingfish come in to feed on them. Fishing with heavy livebait rods baited with live mullet will stimulate action from schools of kingfish. Catching the mullet can be the hardest part of this technique; innovative local anglers use large green poppers that imitate female mullet, which they slowly retrieve to draw amorous male mullet within range. Other anglers then cast a jagging rig of three or four treble hooks over the top of the pursuing mullet and foul-hook them. Care needs to be taken when catching mullet like this as hooks fly in all directions.

South Head

The south head of the Manukau Harbour is the most productive surfcasting spot of the whole region. It does involve quite a drive out through Waiuku and then on to the signal station on Hartner Road, followed by a 400 m scramble down a steep, loose clay and sandstone face. This is a spot for fit anglers as the hike back up is a killer. Always take plenty of fluids with you on this journey.

The long beach on the inside of the heads is where fishing is best, with plenty of gurnard, trevally, kahawai and spotted dogfish. The key to success here is a good cast to put baits into the channel and break-out sinkers to hold firm in the strong current. The best time to fish is during a southeasterly wind, two hours either side of full tide.

Best baits
Live mullet
Salted bonito
Mullet
Pilchard

Recommended fishing gear
15 kg trace
50 kg trace
8/10 kg boat outfit
6 kg jig set
3/0 circle hooks
4/0 suicide hooks
10/0 livebaiting hooks
2/0 pink flasher rigs
Small rubber tail jigs
40–200 g teardrop sinker

Boat fishing on the Manukau

Boat fishing on the Manukau is very productive with lots of gurnard and kahawai present most of the time, and trevally and snapper showing up seasonally. Not to mention kingfish and sharks that quite often surprise anglers by taking baits aimed at smaller species.

The whole concept of fishing the Manukau involves using the tidal flow and banks to the angler's benefit. As the tide floods, fish move up on to the banks and channel edges to feed. When the tide recedes, accompanied by the stronger currents, the fish move into the deeper channels and areas where they do not have to fight the current so much. Bites times are controlled primarily by the state of the tide. Anchor in the right spot and you will get bites.

Gurnard are plentiful in the Manukau Harbour.

The Northern Channel runs close to shore in the area from Blockhouse Bay to Cornwallis and is marked by channel buoys. Fish just on the inside of the channel on the edge of the mud banks in 4–8 m of water on a rising tide. Kahawai and gurnard will bite freely. The further up towards Cornwallis you fish, the better the results will be.

Just inside the channel at Puponga Point is a mussel bed that is very productive and sheltered in southwest and northerly winds.

When winds are in the west and southwest on the Manukau, fishing on the Waiuku Channel offers plenty of scope. Launch sites at Waiau Pa and

Te Toro offer good access to this side of the Manukau Harbour, which is protected by the Awhitu Peninsula.

Fishing techniques are the same as for the other side of the harbour. Anchoring on the edge of the banks off Matakawau Point right up to Big Bay will see gurnard, kahawai and school-size snapper caught. The best rig is a 2/0 to 3/0 flasher rig baited with bonito or pilchard. Changing sinker weights to match the speed of the current will extend your fish catching time at each spot. And moving to the lower current areas on the outgoing tide will see fish coming aboard on both sides of the tide. Keep baits small to avoid the sharks and rays that abound in this area.

Berleying is very effective, but on the Manukau it can attract an overabundance of kahawai and small sharks if you're targeting gurnard and snapper.

Targeting trevally in the Manukau requires a slightly different approach. The best areas to fish are off the mussel banks off Huia or inside the current on Puponga Point, Destruction Gully and Mako Point by Big Bay. The odd one will be caught as a bycatch on gurnard rigs. But using mussels for berley and tuatua and mussel for bait rigged on a small 3/0 suicide hooks will routinely tempt shy-biting trevally. Fish with 6 kg rods with fine tips and plenty of grunt down low for this species, which averages 2–4 kg here.

Travel towards the Manukau Heads and anchor on the last channel marker before the bar and you're on one of the best snapper spots in the harbour. In the middle of the harbour between Cake Island and Huia, this spot is best on an incoming tide when the wind is light from the east.

Fish with a heavily weighted running rig or ledger rig baited with mullet. It can also be worth putting out a second rod baited with whole piper, mullet or flounder because kingfish are caught here on bottom baits regularly over summer and autumn.

Look to the south side of the harbour from the channel marker and you will see a little rock called Cake or Tipitai Island. Cake Island is hit by the current on both tides, creating a natural bait pool where predators ambush prey. While it is not a good place to anchor and fish, trolling with kahawai or kingfish lures, as well as livebaits, is well worth the effort. Note: you can also walk onto Cake Island from Wattle Bay at low tide.

On calm days when light easterlies have held sway for a couple of days, it is possible to cross the Manukau Bar in pleasure boats. This is best left to experienced boaties travelling in the company of another boat.

Crossing the bar should always be done at the top or bottom of the tide, as even on calm days large pressure waves are formed by the current hitting the shallow sandbar.

Once over the Manukau Bar the fishing is very productive. There is not a great deal of structure on the bottom so fish anywhere there is a change in the contour or signs of school fish.

Best baits

Live kahawai
Salted bonito
Pilchard
Squid
Fillets of mullet

Recommended fishing gear

15/24 kg stand-up set up
10 kg boat outfit
24 kg trace
100 kg trace
6/0 circle hooks
10/0 livebaiting hooks
5/0 flashers
Small squid lures rigged with a double hook
Green and yellow game lures

Once over the bar, travel out to 35–40 m deep water and drift-fish with 5/0 flashers or strayline rigs for large gurnard and kahawai. From October onwards large schools of snapper are also present in this area with 5–10 kg fish being commonplace.

In January, schools of albacore, skipjack and yellowfin tuna move in on the waters just behind the bar, accompanied by striped marlin. Trolling large and small game lures anywhere from a few hundred metres behind the bar to 30 nautical miles out to sea can produce exceptional gamefishing.

A good day over the bar is to be relished as they don't happen that often, though when they do, the results are seldom disappointing.

Looking back to the Manukau Bar and Whatipu.

Coromandel Peninsula

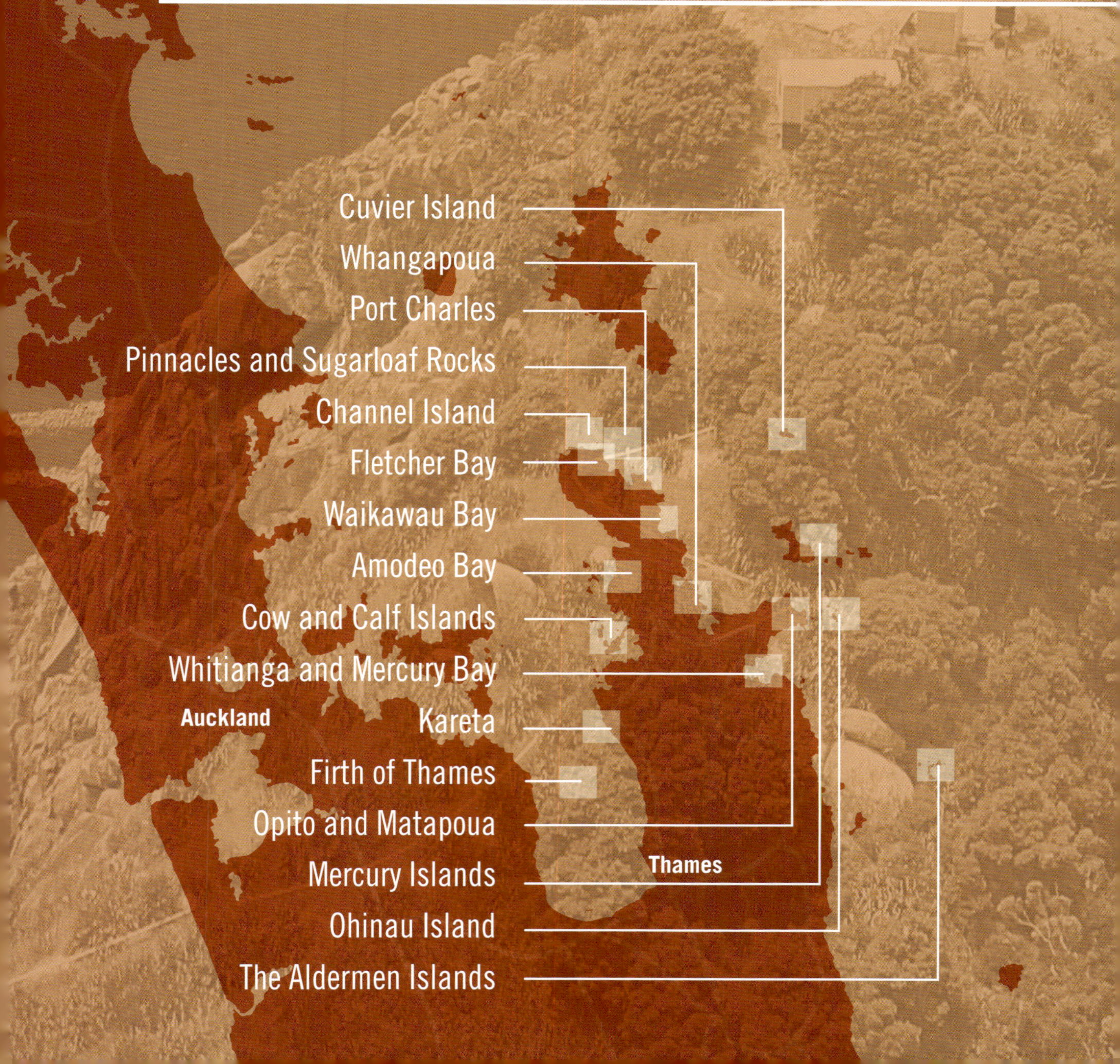

Cuvier Island

Whangapoua

Port Charles

Pinnacles and Sugarloaf Rocks

Channel Island

Fletcher Bay

Waikawau Bay

Amodeo Bay

Cow and Calf Islands

Whitianga and Mercury Bay

Auckland

Kareta

Firth of Thames

Opito and Matapoua

Mercury Islands

Thames

Ohinau Island

The Aldermen Islands

Coromandel Peninsula

East of Auckland is the Coromandel Peninsula with the spectacular Coromandel and Moehau Ranges. It is a popular area for holidaymakers and tourists. Rich in gold-mining history and with a variety of landscapes, the Coromandel Peninsula is also rich in fishing hotspots for boaties and shore-based anglers.

The tip of the Coromandel Peninsula faces north and it has extensive east and west coasts. On the west side the shallow waters of the Firth of Thames extend up into the Hauraki Gulf, while on the eastern side golden sandy beaches and bays are broken up by a rocky coastline that falls away into the Pacific Ocean.

The quickest route to the Coromandel Peninsula is via State Highway 2 and then onto State Highway 25. This will lead to the small town of Kopu, which is 100 km from Auckland. From Kopu, directions are signposted for both sides of the peninsula.

Firth of Thames

The west coast road follows the coast to the top of the peninsula and is long and winding. Crossing over to the east coast is best through the Kopu-Hikuai Road on State Highway 25A, especially if you are towing a boat.

The Firth of Thames, on the western shore, fishes well seasonally when snapper move in to spawn from November onwards. Launch sites at Tapu and Kareta are popular. A short run to the edge of the channel, where water depth is 10 m, will put you onto the fish. Fish the rising tide with berley set on the bottom and rig with a single 4/0 suicide hook and a 25 g ball sinker right on the hook. Baits like pilchard, mullet and squid all work well in this area.

Off Kareta there is a series of mussel farms that are great areas to target snapper and big kingfish. During mussel harvesting, the sea can go red with snapper feeding on the mussels broken while being processed. Jigging with 60–90 g lures under the birds that are often seen working the area can produce nice snapper and John dory.

North of Te Kouma and Manaia Harbours, the Cow and Calf Islands sit in front of the entrance to Coromandel Harbour. These islands signal the transition from the Firth of Thames to the Hauraki Gulf. Water colour and clarity improve from here, getting better the further up you go along the clusters of islands and reefs that follow the coast right up to the Black Rocks off the Happy Jack Islands.

Prospecting around the Happy Jacks can produce some big fish.

This region offers plenty of fishing options. The techniques for fishing the reefs and islands are all similar. Fish in the deeper channels between the islands or fish back onto the semi-submerged reefs with straylined baits. Berley will draw fish in the area you are fishing and a rising tide at dusk will see fish moving in very close to the rocks to feed on kina, mussels and baitfish.

Large kingfish hunt in this territory all year and can be targeted with a floating piper bait or live kahawai rigged under a balloon. Landing on these islands can be a really good option as large snapper and trevally can be targeted off the rocks where they move in to feed. Pick a spot that falls away into deep water or where you can cast into a gutter or channel between rocks.

On the mainland, the surfcasting from Amodeo Bay north improves significantly due to the deeper water closer in and the rocky terrain. Surfcasters should pick a headland that gives access to deep water and current. Fish with whole pilchards, piper or mullet baits. There is no

Travelling the Coromandel Peninsula is best taken slowly as the roads can be rugged and do get flooded in heavy rain. Accommodation should be booked in advance. No fuel is available north of Colville Store.

need to use sinkers any larger than 100 g as long casts are not important because snapper tend to move in on the rising tide.

Just past Colville, the last place to get fuel before the top of the peninsula, you come to a fork in the road. One way heads to Port Jackson, the other to Port Charles. The sealed roads also finish at this point and gravel roads can get dusty in summer and flooded in heavy rain. Stay on the western route and you will come to the small camp area at Fantail Bay. This is an idyllic spot with pohutukawa trees and an area to launch small boats and kayaks.

Successful boat fishing can quite simply be a matter of moving straight off the camp where the bottom drops away to 20–30 m deep. A standard running rig with sinkers between 50–100 g works well. The other good option is fishing back into the reefs where snapper, kahawai and kingfish reside. Whole piper is particularly good bait, either live or dead, and is best fished with a two-hook rig with no sinker.

Rock fishing on the point just north of the camp works well; use a standard surfcasting rig and also put out a live piper under a small float to tempt the many kingfish that patrol the coast.

Travelling on, you will pass Port Jackson and come to Fletcher Bay and a Department of Conservation campsite. The boat and shore fishing here are some of the most productive on the whole of the Coromandel, with Port Jackson Reef and Square Top Island being the prime spots for boat fishermen.

Tidal currents here can get up to three knots and create rough seas even on calm days. The rocks all around Fletcher Bay, and if you don't mind a bit of a walk, the Pinnacles and Sugarloaf Rocks, offer premium platforms with good, deep water and strong currents right at your feet. It is best to walk around the rocks at low tide and return on the outgoing tide.

Big snapper and huge kingfish hunt in this area all year. Serious rock fishing tackle is required to handle the sort of fish you will encounter here. A solid, 3-m rock-casting rod suitable for 10–15 kg line and capable of casting unweighted snapper baits and poppers is recommended, along with another rig for livebaiting live kahawai – this rig should have a rating of 15 kg plus.

Straight off Cape Colville lies remote Channel Island. This spot fulfills all the requirements for a fantastic possie. The structure rises out of deep water and is hit by strong currents of highly oxygenated water, home to loads of feed. Boats can go to Channel Island from Auckland, Great Barrier Island and either side of Coromandel Peninsula. It's a fair hike across the water from Auckland – approximately 150 km round trip – so ensure your boat has the range and is equipped to handle offshore runs of this nature.

Channel Island has one main exposed island and a smaller exposed reef off to one side, while sub-surface a long reef stretches to the west. The gut between the island and the reef is the prime straylining area. Big baits of whole skipjack heads or kahawai fillets are scoffed by double-figure snapper.

The southern face of Channel Island, where the depth is 40–45 m, is good for kingfish jigging. Often large schools of kingfish will bust up through baitfish on the surface. Fishing with mackerel and kahawai livebaits, weighted so they stay deep, will attract strikes from the larger kingfish that inhabit Channel Island.

Bottom fishing in the deeper water for tarakihi, snapper and trevally with baited flasher rigs is good all around the island, as long as you fish on a piece of structure.

The camping ground at Rocky Bay has good facilities.

The Pinnacles produce snapper and kingfish.

Port Charles is on the eastern side of the Coromandel Peninsula and is very remote, so it pays to take all your provisions if you are planning a trip there. There are a few homes and baches for rent and a good Department of Conservation camping ground at Rocky Bay.

Boats of 3–6 m can be launched at one of the small bays, or Sandy Bay off the beach with the help of a 4WD or tractor. It is also possible to launch boats up to 4 m at Rocky Bay if your four-wheel-driving skills are good. Port Charles is a good base if you want to boat fish the Pinnacles and Channel Island. Dozens of good spots are within minutes of launching.

The deep water all around Lion Rock, on the southern side of the bay, fishes well for a variety of species with a constant berley trail. Big kingfish abound around the points and reefs in the Port Charles region and can be caught all year, with April and May regularly producing fish exceeding

Best baits

Live kahawai

Skipjack

Tuatua

Pilchard

Piper

Sprat

Recommended fishing gear

Surfcasting rig

15/24 kg stand-up set up

8/10 kg boat outfit

6 kg jig set

100 kg trace

12/0 circle hooks

5/0 suicide hooks

10/0 livebaiting hooks

2/0–5/0 flashers

250–1000 g hapuku sinkers

Waikawau Beach is a picture-postcard spot.

30 kg. Fishing with live kahawai trolled slowly behind the boat or fished off the rocks under a balloon is the best way to attract these monsters.

A small mussel farm right in Port Charles is a good spot to fish. It will produce snapper, kahawai, trevally and John dory. Anchor in front of the mussel farm on an incoming tide and fish with a lightly weighted strayline rig. Pilchards and squid baits work well and groundbaiting the area will stimulate the fish to feed.

Heading back from Port Charles there is a small diversion that takes you a little way down the east coast before it heads back over to the west. Here you will come to Waikawau Bay. Serviced by a large camping ground, the absolutely beautiful golden sand beach offers small boat launching with 4WD vehicles when calm. Casting a surf rod off the beach will produce kahawai and the odd snapper.

Te Anaputa Point to the north offers the best fishing for kahawai and snapper. There is also quite a bit of reef just south of Waikawau Bay between Kokumata and Pukenui Points – worth berleying and fishing with pilchard baits.

Crossing to the eastern shore of the Coromandel Peninsula, holiday areas are set up around the many golden sand beaches from Whangamata up to Whangapoua Harbour, with lots of motels, camping grounds and beach accommodation.

Some of these areas are quite built-up and exclusive. None-the-less, they offer superb fishing. Boat launching facilities on the east coast of the Coromandel are fairly good, with many concrete ramps and deepwater launch sites. There are a couple of spots where river and harbour bars need to be negotiated, but in good conditions these present few problems.

While the coast has good spots to fish, the big drawcard is the offshore islands and reefs that run all down the coast. Cuvier, the Mercury group and The Aldermen Islands offer spectacular reef fishing for snapper, trevally and kingfish with deepwater reefs that produce hapuku, bluenose and tarakihi when sea conditions are favourable.

Inshore, Ohinau Island, Flat Island and The Black Rocks are the best areas to catch big snapper, kahawai and trevally. When gamefishing was in its infancy in New Zealand, this area, generally known as Mercury Bay, was one of the main areas fished. Today, marlin, tuna and sharks are still caught regularly during summer.

Fishing on the eastern side of the Coromandel Peninsula is good all year with winter and spring producing the best hapuku, tarakihi and trevally. From October onwards, snapper and kingfish move inshore prior to spawning.

Because of the diversity of the fishing, it pays to have a good variety of tackle for inshore, offshore and deepwater fishing. Drifting over the vast sandy bottom areas just off the beaches will produce a feed of gurnard at most times.

Plenty of good rock and beach options exist for shore-based fishemen. The wharf at Whitianga is a good spot to take the kids to catch sprats and piper. John dory can be caught using livebaits on a ledger rig dropped around the piles.

At the end of Whangapoua, a short hike out to the rocky headland is a good spot to fish for snapper and kahawai. Freshly-caught piper and sprats, cast out with no sinker, will tend to produce the larger fish.

The area off Opito and Matapoua is popular for kayak fishing, with anglers using kayaks to get to the rocks. Here big snapper and kingfish hunt the washes and gutters on the islands. Berleying off the rocks will attract kahawai and snapper right to your feet. Baits should be rigged on 50 kg trace with a single 7/0 baited with whole pilchards or pieces of kahawai fillet. Kingfish willingly devour kahawai livebaits and fresh piper cast and retrieved just below the surface.

The best way to approach fishing the Coromandel Penninsula is to base yourself close to where you want to fish and be prepared for a bit of travelling to areas where the conditions are best. You can find a fishable spot within an hour of all the areas listed. The worst wind is a northerly – this can create a swell running down both coasts.

Tauranga Harbour

Mayor Island

Pukehina Beach and
Kohioawa Beach

Rurima Islands

Moutohora or Whale Island

Whakatane

White Island

Cape Runaway

Tauranga

Opotiki

Rotorua

Bay of Plenty

The Bay of Plenty has hundreds of kilometres of white sand surf beaches and large offshore islands rising to the surface from the depths of the Pacific. A mild climate means the fishing is good all year round.

Tauranga and Mount Maunganui are located only two and a half hours' drive from Auckland following State Highway 2. Whakatane is a further one and a half hours down the coast from Tauranga, turning off at State Highway 30.

The Bay of Plenty's fishing waters extend from the beaches to the offshore islands, offering an abundance of fish species. World-record kingfish and snapper have been caught in the Bay of Plenty area. The Bay is also well serviced by fishing charters, with Mayor Island and White Island being the most popular destinations.

Boat launching is good around Tauranga, Mt Maunganui and Whakatane. A large charter fleet operates in the Bay of Plenty, offering half-day and day trips or long range, live-aboard adventures.

Dawn and dusk are the best times to fish the beach.

Shore fishing

For anglers who enjoy surfcasting or setting kontikis, the beaches that stretch from Papamoa right down to Whakatane are ideal. Gurnard and kahawai are the mainstays, while snapper and trevally turn up seasonally.

With such a lot of shoreline, where to actually fish can be daunting. The more popular and productive spots are along Pukehina Beach and Kohioawa Beach by Matata – also the entrances to the small estuaries that are dotted down the coast.

The time of day and baits used play a big part in what anglers are likely to catch off the beaches. Cast out half a pilchard during the day and the odd kahawai may be the only capture. Fish at sunset and into the night and snapper become less timid, coming closer to the beach to feed. Use shellfish for bait and the number of trevally captured will increase. And the areas where the shellfish were gathered are good places to fish. Quite often this will be on the edge of one of the estuary channels.

Best baits

Live mackerel

Skipjack

Tuatua

Pilchard

Squid

Mullet

Salted bonito

Recommended fishing gear

Surfcasting rig

15/24 kg stand-up set

8/10 kg boat outfit

6 kg jig set

100 kg trace

12/0 circle hooks

5/0 suicide hooks

10/0 livebaiting hooks

2/0–5/0 flashers

250–1000 g ball and hapuku sinkers

Gurnard really like salted bonito and are easy to target when the water is not too rough. They will feed just behind the breakers. It has become very popular to add small floats to surf rigs as the beaches have a healthy population of paddle crabs.

Kontiki fishing is best when the wind is from the west to northwest. Mullet and salted bonito are the best baits as crabs rip soft baits to pieces before they get past the breakers.

Boat fishing

Tauranga Harbour is the handiest launch site for fishing the northern Bay of Plenty. The harbour has two mouths at either end of Matakana Island, which stretches from Katikati to Mount Maunganui. Fishing inside the harbour can be good and is a sensible option if the seas are too rough to venture offshore.

Trolling a bibbed minnow through the harbour entrances is a good start to your fishing day. Kingfish often hang around the rocks at the Mount Maunganui end and just behind the bar at Bowentown.

Bibbed minnows dive and have a strong swimming action.

Mayor Island

On leaving the harbour, Mayor Island lies just to the north and is normally visible. On the way out to Mayor there is a patch of reef – the Penguin Shoals. It is one of the reasons the Bay of Plenty's fishing is so productive. The currents that push up and down the coast hit these patches of reefs and islands, forcing krill and plankton to the surface where fish feed on them. This food chain follows the natural progression with big fish eating the smaller ones.

On the Penguin Shoals and Astrolabe Reef huge schools of kahawai, trevally and maomao feed freely. Casting small lures or saltwater flies amongst the schooling fish will provoke a response. Pink- and chrome-coloured lures work very well.

Bottom fishing close to the reefs will produce snapper, tarakihi and reef fish, while livebaiting catches kingfish and even marlin.

In the late winter albacore of up to 25 kg move into the Bay of Plenty and can be caught trolling with small game lures no more than 10 cm long. Likewise, when the water warms to 18 to 19°C, skipjack and yellowfin tuna move into the same areas to feed in the food-rich waters.

Mayor Island is an extinct volcano and has safe overnight anchorages for boats of all sizes. Part of the island is a marine reserve with restrictions on fishing, so check your chart before wetting a line.

On the south side of the island Tuhua Reef, a very popular spot to target kingfish, is renowned as a monster snapper spot. The best technique for big snapper is to anchor close to the reef structure and strayline with whole mackerel baits and piper cast into the shallow washes.

Kingfish respond well to livebaits fished under a balloon or fished deep. Moving on to the deeper part of Tuhua Reef, tarakihi and reef fish bite on flasher rigs baited with squid or shellfish.

A few kilometres off the south and eastern sides of Mayor Island the water becomes very deep with substantial bottom structure. Dropping heavy-duty ledger rigs with medium-sized circle hooks and slabs of squid, barracouta or bonito will attract the attention of hapuku, ling, bluenose and bass.

Best baits

Live mackerel
Skipjack
Tuatua
Pilchard
Squid
Barracouta

Recommended fishing gear

Surfcasting rig
15/24 kg stand-up set
8/10 kg boat outfit
6 kg jig set
100 kg trace
12/0 circle hooks
5/0 suicide hooks
10/0 livebaiting hooks
2/0–5/0 flashers
250–1000 g ball and hapuku sinkers

To get onto a rock that is holding fish, it is necessary to set up the boat drift in the right direction to cope with wind and tide. Random fishing in this area is fruitless and local knowledge and a powerful fish finder are essential.

Motiti Island is 23 km offshore and can be accessed by boat or plane. Lodge-style accommodation is available on the island. Fishing off the rocks has produced plenty of huge snapper and kingfish. A small inflatable or kayak can be handy to reach some of the more isolated points. Scuttled just a few metres off Motiti, the wreck of the Taioma is worth a look. Boat fishing possies are plentiful around the exposed reef structure. Strayline fishing and livebaiting are the favoured techniques.

Strayline rigs are simple and effective for fishing in the shallows. Sinker weight should be adjusted to suit the current.

Whakatane

The fishing off Whakatane is without doubt world-class, and I have never been disappointed when fishing these waters – the diversity of species, amazing scenery and the great onshore facilities can't be faulted. Whakatane has the distinction of being the yellowfin tuna capital of New Zealand, with the annual yellowfin tournament attracting up to 800 anglers.

On days of high volcanic activity, a plume of smoke and steam rises from White Island, offering an awe-inspiring view of one of the great forces of nature.

Whakatane township is signposted on State Highway 2 turning to State Highway 30, some four hours from Auckland and about one hour's drive from Rotorua on State Highway 34.

Where the Whakatane River runs to the sea, the entrance or bar can be difficult and caution should be exercised during crossings. Daily updates of tide times, the marine forecast, outlook, and sea and swell conditions are indicated on a whiteboard at the boat ramp. The Whakatane Volunteer Coastguard also broadcasts the status of the bar, along with the marine forecast and outlook during the scheduled transmission times on VHF channel 84.

After crossing the bar, the first spots are close at hand with the rocks to the right of the mouth turning on snapper and kahawai. Fishing on the sand, either anchored or drifting, a kilometre or so off the bar will produce plenty of big, fat gurnard. Fish with 3/0 flasher rigs baited with salted bonito. A trick when gurnard fishing is to use long, thin strips of bait and allow the gurnard time to eat up to the hook.

Moutohora or Whale Island, as it is locally known, is located 9.6 km off the coast of Whakatane, giving you the opportunity to fish clear water teeming with fish. Public access to the island is restricted to permit holders, approved tour parties and senior school groups.

Inshore fishing at Whale Island will produce snapper and the sheltered bays are good for catching mackerel livebaits at dawn and dusk. There are areas that hold tarakihi in 30–40 m just off the island. Looking at a chart or talking to the local tackle store owners will reveal the co-ordinates.

When the water temperature rises above 18°C, skipjack and yellowfin tuna can be found schooling. Trolling with small pink squid lures or 4/0 saltwater flies will catch the skipjack, while yellowfin can be targeted by

The boat ramp at Whakatane is suitable for boats of all sizes and can be used at all stages of the tide.

Best baits
Salted bonito
Mackerel livebaits

Recommended
fishing gear
15 kg jig set
3/0 flasher rigs
Pink squid lures
2/0–4/0 livebait hooks
30–60 kg fluorocarbon trace
Bibbed minnows
4/0 saltwater flies
Medium-sized game lures

trolling medium-sized game lures at 5–7 knots. The easiest way to get onto the tuna is to follow the gannets and dolphins.

In some seasons large schools of baitfish, such as anchovies and pilchards, come into the eastern Bay of Plenty. These bait schools get herded up by the predators, forming what is known as a meatball. If you can find a meatball there is a good chance the baitfish will take station under your boat for protection from diving birds. They're still vulnerable to attack from below, but this behaviour gives anglers the chance to scoop baitfish in a fine-mesh landing net and use them for bait and live berley to keep the predators around.

I've had days meatballing when schools of yellowfin tuna in the 15–40 kg class could be hooked pretty much at will. The best tackle for this style of fishing is a 15 kg heavy jig set with a mid-size lever-drag reel. Use small 2/0 to 4/0 livebait hooks on 30–60 kg fluorocarbon trace.

East of Whale Island and 16 km from Whakatane lie the Rurima Islands. This is a group of three small islands and in the sea around them volcanic gas bubbles can be seen. The main island is called Rurima, to the west is Tokata and to the east Moutoki.

The islands are covered in pohutukawa trees and Rurima Island has two sandy bays. One kilometre separates the two main island groups, made up of shallow water dotted with reef structure. These waters are prime snapper and kingfish country.

A good berley trail set close to the rocks will bring in the snapper. Size can vary from pan-sized up to 10 kg plus. This is the kind of place where a hot bite can develop to the stage where all the fish are big.

Kingfish take surface-fished livebaits and trolled bibbed minnows.

White Island on one of its less active days.

White Island

One of the unique aspects of the eastern Bay of Plenty is fishing at White Island, an active volcano. Veiws of the sulphurous crater and relics of the old mine can be seen on the southwestern side of the island.

The fishing at White Island cannot be categorised because of the abundance of species available. The best way to deal with White Island is by summarising the main techniques used to catch fish.

Close in to the island are many reefs and kelp forests. Using a 10 kg boat set rigged with a ledger rig or small flasher rig is the best way to target the tarakihi, trevally and reef fish. Squid, shellfish and fresh skipjack are the favoured baits.

White Island has some of the largest kingfish in the world. They're mostly caught deep livebaiting with mackerel, flying fish and koheru. Fifteen kg plus stand-up game tackle is considered light for this tough fishing. Terminal rigs are made up using an arm's length of 80 kg mono, a 12/0 circle hook and 200–300 g of ball sinkers above a ballbearing swivel.

Fishing with livebait will produce huge kingfish around White Island.

High-speed jigging is another technique for targeting kingfish. In recent times the trend has been to use 15 kg jig tackle with long, thin jigs weighing 150–400 g. These are rigged with a single hook with either a heavy split ring or braid cord. Jigs are lowered to the bottom or cast and allowed to sink, then retrieved as fast as possible.

Kingfish can be found all around White Island, from the Volkner Rocks,

5 km to the north, to the Club Rocks close to the island itself. During spring, surface activity increases as the kingies chase pelagic baitfish called saury. Fishing under any bird activity is always productive when this happens. During quieter times the kingfish hold up on reefs in 40–100 m.

The current world-record kingfish – at a massive 53 kg – was caught here. Local charter boats have been proactive in conservation, introducing a one kingfish per angler per day limit to protect this amazing fishery for future generations. With such an abundance of good eating fish, this is recommended for visitors to the region also.

White Island trenches, deepwater reefs and knolls are home to many deepwater species of fish like hapuku, bluenose and bass. Winter and spring are the best times to target these deepwater fish. The technique involves drifting over the trenches and dropping heavy ledger rigs to the depths. Stand-up game rods spooled with 600–800 m of 24–37 kg non-stretch braid line are best. The depths fished can be up to 300 m!

This form of fishing involves a fair bit of muscle and winding when a 30 kg hapuku is hooked. A good rod gimbal and harness are essential.

Many tuna species, striped, blue and black marlin, mahi mahi, spearfish and sharks are all present in the blue water currents around White Island. Gamefishing starts in late November and runs through to May; 24 kg plus stand-up game tackle is the usual choice.

A run of large albacore starts in May and is usually finished in July.

Fishing with big game tackle, trolling game lures and large skipjack livebaits following the current lines and baitfish schools is the way to target the fish that travel the ocean's warm currents.

Fishing buddy Cecil Alexander with a nice hapuku.   Photo: Cecil Alexander.

Opotiki and East Cape

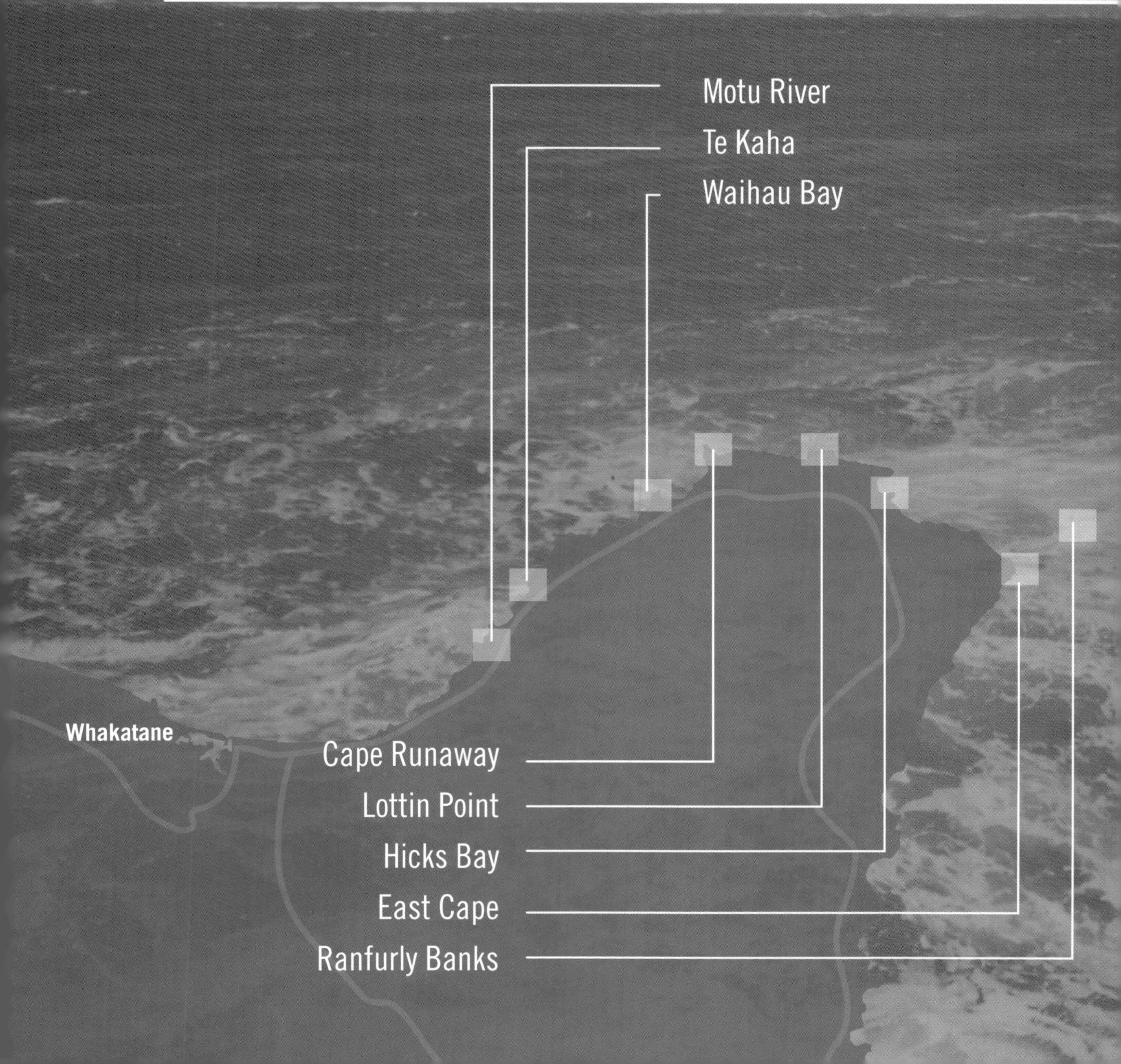

Motu River

Te Kaha

Waihau Bay

Whakatane

Cape Runaway

Lottin Point

Hicks Bay

East Cape

Ranfurly Banks

Motu River

A good tell-tale sign that there is some action here is the number of cars parked at the river mouth.

Best baits

Pilchard

Recommended fishing gear

Surfcasting rig
24 kg trace
5/0 suicide hooks
Break-out sinkers
100 g chrome lures

Travel east of Whakatane and take State Highway 35 from Opotiki. This route follows the coast road around the Bay of Plenty towards East Cape. Sandy surf beaches give way to shingle bays and a rocky coastline and there is less available in the way of accommodation and facilities.

The Motu River, 40 km out of Opotiki, has an annual run of whitebait. These transparent baitfish are eagerly devoured by massive schools of kahawai as they enter the mouth of the river.

Fishing with surfcasters rigged with a simple 100 g chrome lure cast across the river and rapidly retrieved will invoke strike after strike from the hard-fighting kahawai.

This run usually occurs any time from September through to late November. The flooding tide seems to be the best time to fish in the area just inside the river mouth.

Using light spinning tackle adds a new dimension to catching kahawai.

Te Kaha

The small settlement of Te Kaha is a further 35 km up the road from the Motu River. Te Kaha is a popular place to launch boats, although it can be a bit tricky with lots of little reefs to navigate. A bit of local help can be very handy.

The bottom fishing out from Te Kaha ranges from good to outstanding. The two main reasons are the vast areas of submerged reef and the XOS snapper that are caught here. Tarakihi, gurnard, kahawai, kingfish and hapuku are also common captures and the depth of the reef plays a part in which species you catch, because hapuku and tarakihi prefer deeper, cooler water.

The big snapper move onto the reefs around Te Kaha in late December and can be found right through until late April. Early on, locating the travelling schools on a fishfinder and drifting through them with pilchard baits weighted to hold the bottom is the best technique.

Later, the big snapper then take up residence on the reefs in 20–50 m of water and berleying on a rising tide at change of light will attract bites.

Pilchards and squid are the most effective baits rigged on a pair of 6/0 suicide hooks.

The offshore gamefishing is also very good from late January onwards. The area around 220 m deep sees a lot of big blue marlin that really test an angler's skills. Yellowfin can be found within a couple of kilometres from shore and anchoring and fishing mackerel livebaits and pilchard cubes yields good success. Throw in a couple of pilchard cubes every 30 seconds or so for berley.

Te Kaha has shops, fuel and accommodation. The best winds are from the southeast. A ramp permit may be required. 4WD vehicles are recommended for launching purposes.

Best baits
Pilchard
Squid
Live mackerel
Skipjack

Recommended fishing gear
15/24 kg livebait set up
8/10 kg boat set
100 kg trace
12/0 circle hooks
6/0 suicide hooks
6/0 livebaiting hooks
2/0–5/0 flashers

Using a two-hook rig is good when fishing large baits.

Use small extra-strong hooks for cubing.

Waihau Bay to 🎣 🎣 East Cape

State Highway 35 continues to travel east from Te Kaha along the coast. The very scenic drive reveals many easily accessed bays and headlands that offer good rock fishing for snapper, kahawai and kingfish. For divers with a good set of lungs, it is also possible to snorkel for crayfish off the rocks during summer.

Robust, mid-size, lever-drag reels are ideal for tuna and kingfish.

Waihau Bay is about 50 km from Te Kaha and 140 km from Whakatane. Geographically it is a good base for anglers wanting to fish the prolific waters of Cape Runaway and Lottin Point.

The Waihau Bay area has several camping grounds with caravans, cabins, campsites and a lodge and the Waihau Bay boat ramp is good for easy launching and offers close access to the gamefishing grounds for smaller sportfishing boats.

The fishing around Waihau Bay, like the rest of the area, is very good and on days when the sea is too rough for boating, excellent landbased fishing is close by.

One of the best boat fishing spots is off Cape Runaway. Here the bluewater currents push very close to shore, offering a mixture of pelagic sportfish and bottom fish. Jigging and livebaiting around the Cape Rocks can be fantastic. At times, massive schools of kingfish take offerings with gusto and tear off to the bottom in attempts to bust the angler's line.

Tarakihi, snapper and hapuku are ever-present on the reefs, as well as some of the largest trevally you will find in New Zealand.

Landbased fishing

Around Cape Runaway and heading towards East Cape is New Zealand's easternmost point – Lottin Point. All along this coast the boat fishing is very good, but the major drawcard is the landbased fishing. Huge kingfish, snapper and trevally live close to the rocks and can be targeted easily from the shore.

Lottin Point is accessed by driving to Potaka and following the road out from there. These spots are remote and do require a fair amount of physical fitness to walk to. Any number of rocky ledges offer great fishing platforms and setting up a good berley trail will attract the fish.

The main technique used off the rocks is straylining large, unweighted baits, which works on snapper, trevally and kahawai. Use a 10–15 kg rock rod, single 7/0 hook and a minimum of 24 kg trace.

Livebaiting is the other technique and is used to target kingfish that patrol these waters. Use large kahawai suspended under a party balloon on a 3 m, 60 kg trace. A good rock gaff is essential for landing some of the large fish that can be encountered.

Hicks Bay is tucked a little further around State Highway 35 and offers a little shelter when winds are strong from the northwest. The rocky ledge at the left-hand end of Hicks is a good spot to cast a surf rod with gurnard, kahawai and even a few tarakihi coming into the bay.

If permission is granted by the farm station, access can be gained to a track that leads to Matakoa Point and Midway Point. The walk is not too bad, but is recommended for people of reasonable fitness. Fishing the ledges along this part of the coast, anglers are rewarded with snapper, trevally and kingfish. The techniques are the same as for fishing Lottin Point.

The Waihau Bay area has several camping grounds with caravans, cabins, campsites and a lodge and the Waihau Bay boat ramp is good for easy launching and offers close access to the gamefishing grounds for smaller sportfishing boats.

Best baits
Live kahawai

Recommended fishing gear
24 kg trace
60 kg trace
Rock gaff
10–15 kg rock rod
7/0 hook

Ranfurly Banks

Offshore, wide of East Cape some 16 to 20 nautical miles, the Ranfurly Banks rises up from a depth of 3000 m to only 40 m from the surface. The steep rise of this structure from the sea floor, combined with strong currents, creates a real fishing hotspot.

Many charter boats operate in the area and, as the sea conditions are rarely clam, this is the best way to visit the Ranfurly Banks.

Best baits
Livebaits
Squid
Flying fish

Recommended fishing gear
24–37 kg stand-up tackle
15 kg boat set
Non-stretch dacron
or superbraid line

Sea conditions are rarely calm and the best way to visit the Ranfurly Banks is aboard one of the many charter boats that operate in this area. They have fully equipped boats and expert skippers whose seamanship is needed to undertake a trip to a place as extreme as the Ranfurly Banks.

On a typical visit you can expect to catch hapuku and bass, large kingfish, tarakihi and trumpeter. Trolling to and from the Ranfurly Banks will also produce tuna and marlin.

The techniques for fishing the Ranfurly are not too complicated. Drift-fishing with heavy dropper rigs baited with cut baits or livebaits on 24–37 kg stand-up tackle will handle most of the big fish.

For smaller species, use a slightly down-sized 15 kg rig with smaller hooks on the droppers.

Using non-stretch dacron or superbraid line is a real plus, as it gives the angler the ability to turn fish before they get back to the reef. A full harness with a gimbal belt are also necessary pieces of equipment.

On the subject of gear for the Ranfurly, one skipper put it fairly succinctly when he said, "If you're gonna hunt elephants, don't bring a peashooter."

Heavy duty tackle is a must for fishing at Ranfurly Banks.

Gisborne to Hawke's Bay

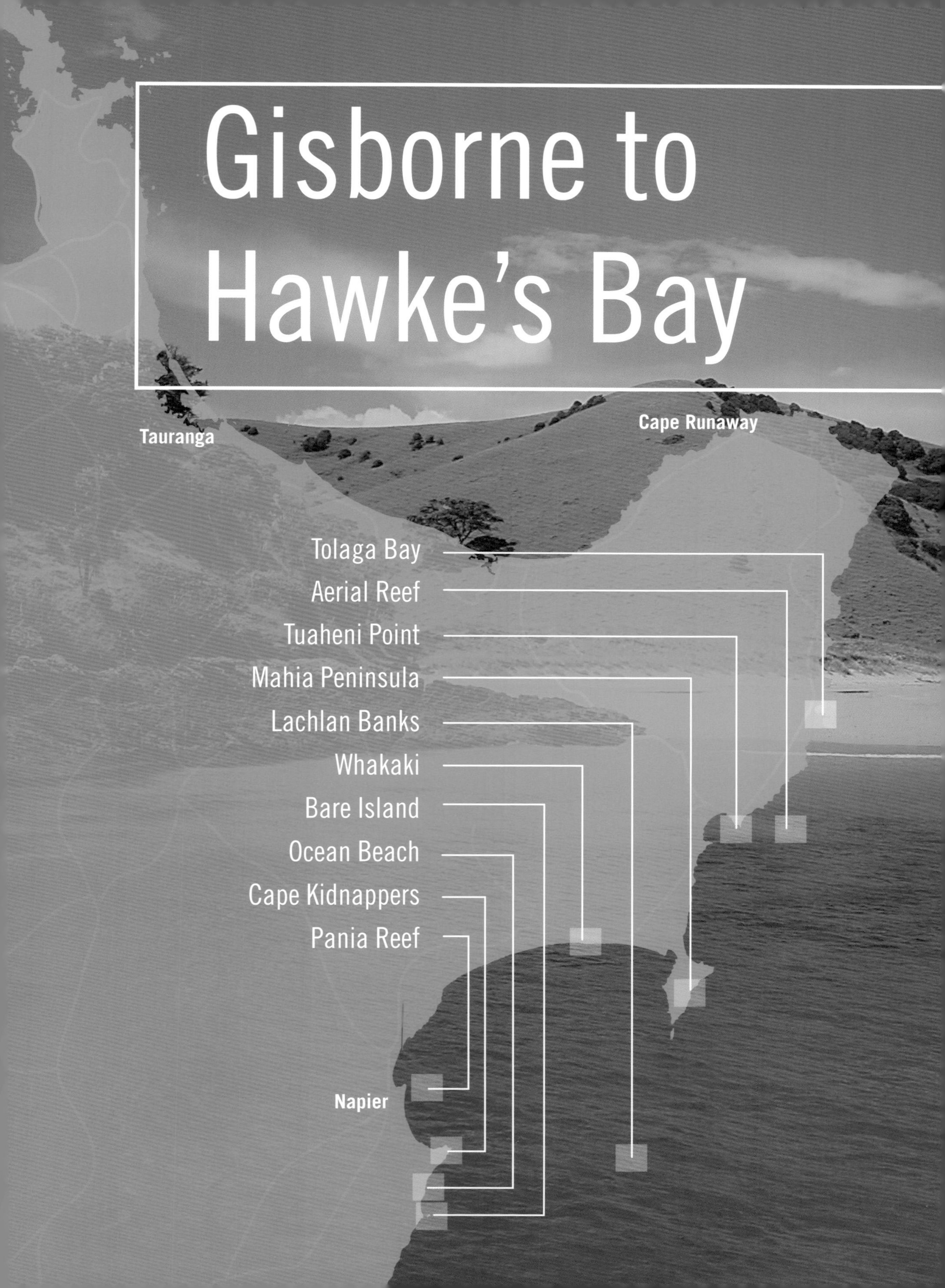

Tauranga

Cape Runaway

Tolaga Bay

Aerial Reef

Tuaheni Point

Mahia Peninsula

Lachlan Banks

Whakaki

Bare Island

Ocean Beach

Cape Kidnappers

Pania Reef

Napier

The region from Gisborne to Hawke's Bay passes some of the more remote parts of the North Island's East Coast. You can follow State Highway 35 around East Cape or take State Highway 2 through the Waioeka Gorge from Opotiki to Gisborne. There are many beaches that offer good surfcasting and plenty of boat fishing opportunities.

Tolaga Bay

Heading back east on State Highway 35 from Gisborne you will pass many good surfcasting beaches and lovely camping grounds.

All the facilities at Tolaga Bay are very good, and it boasts New Zealand's longest wharf.

Best baits

Pilchard
Squid
Live mackerel
Skipjack

Recommended fishing gear

Surfcasting set
10/15 kg jig set
60 kg trace
6/0 suicide hooks
3/0 suicide hooks
2/0–4/0 flashers

Take the signposted turnoff to Tolaga Bay, home to New Zealand's longest wharf. Some 660 m long, this structure is an ideal spot to fish. Cast a surfcaster off the end of the wharf. Fish with a standard running rig and 4/0 hook baited with half a pilchard or strip of bonito, or use baited 4/0 flasher rigs.

The concrete ramp located just inside the river is suitable for most trailer boats and the small river bar is best crossed at high tide.

The fishing is good around the inshore reefs of the Mitre Rocks and Pourewa Island. Crayfish can be found in very shallow water during summer and it is possible to catch them while snorkelling. Offshore, Tolaga Reef is to the north about 45 km off the coast. A good variety of species are caught here including hapuku, kingfish, blue cod and tarakihi.

A kingfish caught at Tolaga Reef, tagged and ready for release.

Aerial Reef

Sitting 10 km southeast of Tatapouri, close to the continental shelf, this expansive reef, ranging in depth from 10 to 40 m, is renowned for its game and bottom fishing.

Aerial Reef is one of the East Coast's top diving locations and crayfish are abundant. It is home also to big numbers of seafloor reef fish, mainly tarakihi, blue cod and trumpeter, with snapper seasonally.

When targeting the bottom fish, anchor off the drop-off of the reef in 40–50 m. Use a 4/0 flasher rig baited with squid or skipjack and fish just off the bottom.

Plenty of kingfish hang around the edge of Aerial Reef and it is possible to pick up the schools with a good sounder and drop a jig or livebait to them. During the warmer months tuna and marlin can be caught trolling just off the edge of the reef and along the continental shelf. Launching sites at Tatapouri and Gisborne are suitable for most trailer boats.

Gisborne offers plenty of accommodation, while up the coast Tatapouri has holiday-style accommodation.

Best baits
Pilchard
Squid
Live mackerel
Skipjack

Recommended fishing gear
10/15 kg jig set
60 kg trace
6/0 suicide hooks
2/0–4/0 flashers

Baited flasher rigs work well for bottom fishing around Aerial Reef.

Tuaheni Point

Boat ramps at either Gisborne or Tatapouri are handy to dozens of shallow reefs and holes.

Best baits

Squid
Pilchard
Piper
Salted bonito
Crayfish tail

Recommended fishing gear

Surfcasting set
Ledger rigs
Flashers

The northernmost point of Poverty Bay is a good area for small boats to fish. Boat ramps at either Gisborne or Tatapouri are handy to dozens of shallow reefs and holes.

Fishing with flasher rigs baited with squid is the standard technique here. During summer it is also worth straylining with pilchards and piper baits to target snapper.

Beach fishing in this area is superb. Finding a spot is just a matter of driving up the coast to see which side of the point has the best conditions.

Surfcasting and kontiki fishing both work well and catches include kahawai, gurnard, spotted dogfish and snapper. The two favourite baits for this area are salted bonito and crayfish tail, both of which are tied onto the hook using bait cotton.

Dusk and night fishing are the most productive for snapper and dogfish, while an incoming tide at dawn is good for kahawai and gurnard. The sweep along the beach can be a problem, countered by using break-out surf sinkers.

Young Nicks Head at the southern end of Poverty Bay provides good bottom fishing for snapper, kahawai, blue cod and gurnard. Anchor over the foul straight off the point in 20–30 m. Using berley set on the bottom will definitely improve catches.

Ledger rigs and flashers baited with squid and bonito and fished half a metre or so off the bottom are the best rigs.

Setting berley near the bottom is good if the current is flowing.

Mahia Peninsula

Mahia Peninsula is surrounded by the Pacific Ocean, which breaks onto a mix of black and white sand beaches and rocky beaches. Mahia is a 90-minute drive north from Napier via Wairoa, following State Highway 2. Turn off at Nuhaka, or if you are coming from the Gisborne, take the Morere turnoff. Mahia Peninsula is very popular with holidaymakers and can get very busy over the Christmas and New Year period.

With many beaches and rocky areas, surfcasting and rock fishing will produce everything from kahawai and snapper to kingfish and big sharks. A spot with prevailing offshore winds will fish best.

Fishing with two rods is worthwhile – rig one with standard surf rig; the other should be heavier with 15 kg line and baited with a livebait or large cut bait. This should be fished closer, in deeper channels and gutters.

The most prominent boat fishing spots are Portland Island off the tip of the Mahia Peninsula and Bull Rock, which can be seen breaking the surface on the northeastern side. A wide variety of bottom species are caught at both of these spots.

At times there is a lot of bird and surface activity with schools of kahawai. If encountered, try jigging, trolling and livebaiting among the work-ups. Kingfish and the occasional school of albacore are also found in these areas of activity.

Mahia offers excellent camping spots at Opoutama, Mahia Beach and near Whangawehi Harbour on the eastern side. There are several bed-and-breakfasts, home stays and farm stays within the area. Mahia has a few restaurants and a local pub. Boat launching options are limited and can require the use of a tractor for beach launching.

The best baits

Squid
Pilchard
Live kahawai
Salted bonito
Crayfish tail

Recommended fishing gear

10/15 kg jig set
2x surf set
60 kg trace
7/0 livebait hooks
6/0 long-shank hooks
2/0–4/0 flashers
100 g jigs
Break-out sinkers
Bait cotton

The Mahia Peninsula produces nice snapper seasonally.

Whakaki

Whakaki is not close to any services. Access is easy and suitable for all, requiring only a short walk.

Best baits

Salted bonito
Crayfish tail
Pilchards
Crabs

Recommended fishing gear

2x surf sets
60 kg trace
6/0 long-shank hooks
4/0 suicide hooks
2/0-4/0 flashers
Break-out sinkers
Bait cotton

About halfway between Wairoa and Nuhaka, just past the Whakaki Lagoon, you can access the steep shingle beach of Whakaki. I was introduced to this spot by good friend and surfcasting legend Gary Kemsley, who explained the finer points of fishing here.

The day we fished it was blazing hot and flat calm. We did manage a gurnard and spun up a bunch of kahawai that were working along the beach all day, coming in to casting range occasionally. We also had a kingfish strike on small kahawai livebait fished on a float a few metres from shore. And that was on what Gary considered a bad day!

The prime fishing spot is a channel that runs from the access point to the point at the south of the beach. The best conditions are when there is a bit of a wave break, slightly discoloured water and offshore winds. Big dogfish, gurnard and kahawai are most common, with snapper of all sizes caught from October onwards.

Whakaki, like many of the beaches in this region, does produce a run of large snapper and anglers who put in the hours when the big fish move in will be rewarded with double-figure fish.

The preferred baits for fishing Whakaki are salted bonito, pilchards, crayfish tail and crab. All are bound to the hook with bait elastic. Fish with a distance-casting rig and break-out sinker cast into the channel and with baited flashers on a second outfit fished a little closer to shore.

The best times to fish are on a rising tide. Dogfish bite best after dark and when the water is discoloured.

Spotted dogfish or smooth hounds grow quite large – over 15 kg – and are good eating.

Break-out sinkers with short traces are good for fishing larger baits off the beach.

Pania Reef

Pania Reef is situated 4 km from Napier Wharf. An abundance of species such as kahawai, blue cod and gurnard make it a very popular fishing spot.

The reef is clearly marked and extends for over 1.5 km. The shallowest point is 3 m deep and the reef falls away to over 20 m.

A variety of techniques will work at Pania Reef. The deeper water can be fished with a ledger rig with 50–100 g sinkers. Where the reef shallows, straylining lightly weighted baits down a berley trail is productive.

During summer and autumn, kingfish school on Pania Reef in good numbers. Trolling with bibbed minnows, casting poppers and livebaiting will all catch fish.

Big snapper also make an appearance on Pania Reef from October to December, and then move onto the beaches around Napier prior to spawning. Berleying while drifting with pilchard and squid baits close to the reef can be very effective on snapper that regularly weigh over 9 kg. The ideal conditions are southwest or southeasterly winds that are not too strong. Watch the swell, as the reef can be treacherous if the sea gets up.

Napier is a major centre and has good boat-launching facilities. Accommodation and services are all top-notch.

Best baits
Pilchard
Squid
Mullet
Bonito

Recommended fishing gear
60 kg trace
6/0 long-shank hooks
4/0 suicide hooks
2/0–4/0 flashers
50–150 g teardrop sinkers
14 cm bibbed minnows
Popper
7/0 livebait hooks

Trolling around Pania Reef will produce kingfish.

Lachlan Banks

For the more adventurous anglers, the Lachlan Banks are a 75 km run from Napier and require a GPS and fishfinder to locate. Being situated so far offshore, they are really only an option for larger vessels during good weather.

Charter boats operating out of Napier make trips to the Lachlan Banks. This is definitely a spot for larger boats set up for offshore fishing.

Best baits
Barracouta
Squid
Mullet

Recommended fishing gear
24 kg stand-up rig
100 kg trace
6/0 extra-strong circle hooks
12/0 circle hooks
Gimbal belt
Sea anchor
250–1000 g 'puka leads
Small tuna lures

Due to their remoteness and lack of fishing pressure, the Lachlan Banks produce plenty of fish. All of the deepwater species are here in good numbers, and pelagic predators such as kingfish and albacore are caught mainly in the summer months.

The best fishing is in a depth of 100–130 m along any of the banks. Drift-fishing is the best technique. Setting the course for your drift is very important, as baits need to hit the bottom as quickly as possible. If the drift is too fast, a sea anchor can be handy for holding the boat in position, or use the engine to control the speed of drift.

Stand-up rods with reels spooled with 600 m of 24 kg non-stretch line connected to medium to heavy dropper rigs work well. Use circle hooks small enough for tarakihi and strong enough to hold a big hapuku. Fresh barracouta fillets, squid and other tough baits are preferred.

Trolling small tuna lures to and from the Lachlan Banks is a good way to catch the albacore and other pelagic species that inhabit this area.

The best conditions are when light offshore winds prevail and the swell is a metre or less. The strength of the tidal stream can have an effect on how well the fish bite. Fishing during a medium speed current up to the top of the tide is the most productive.

Circle hooks are ideal for deepwater fishing.

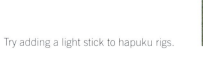

Try adding a light stick to hapuku rigs.

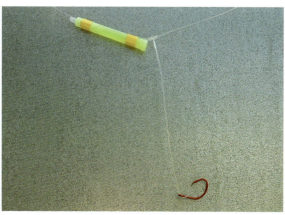

Cape Kidnappers

At the southern end of Hawke Bay is Cape Kidnappers. The gannet colony on the high cliffs of the cape makes a spectacular backdrop for anglers fishing in this area.

There are a number good spots close to the Cape. Black Reef is exposed on the Napier side, Razorback is a submerged line of reef running straight out to sea off Cape Kidnappers and Mercer Rock lies in close proximity to the south. All can be found quite easily with a chart.

The depth range here is between 20 and 90 m, and species range accordingly. It pays to seek a bit of local knowledge as sands shift frequently and cover some of the shallower spots.

Baited flasher rigs will produce blue cod, gurnard and kahawai, while fishing in the deeper water will produce tarakihi, snapper and the odd hapuku.

During the summer months, pelagic gamefish congregate off Cape Kidnappers. The prime area to fish is a few kilometres wide of the Razorback. Trolling for albacore, skipjack and yellowfin tuna at 5–7 knots with 10 cm tuna lures will produce action. Favoured conditions for the Cape are when the winds are in the west and any state of the tide. Fishing is best in the deeper water of the Razorback areas on bright days, while the shallows can be very productive after an onshore blow.

Launching for this spot is best at Clifton, which is signposted from State Highway 2 between Napier and Hastings.

Best baits
Bonito
Squid
Pilchard
Kahawai cut baits

Recommended fishing gear
10/15 kg boat rig
30 kg trace
6/0 suicide hooks
4/0 flasher rigs
10 cm tuna lures

Use lures that are the same size as the baitfish.

Ocean Beach

Ocean Beach is located to the south of Cape Kidnappers and half an hour from Hastings. Travel via Havelock North and follow the signposts. The beautiful, golden sand beach is a popular spot for tourists and surfers.

Havelock North has accommodation and services within half an hour of Ocean Beach. 4WD vehicles can access the beach at the car park.

Best baits

Salted bonito
Pilchard
Kahawai cut baits

Recommended fishing gear

4 m surf rig
30 kg shock leader
4/0 suicide hooks
4/0 flasher rigs
Beach spike
Break-out sinkers
Bait elastic

The beach can be accessed by 4WD vehicles at the car park and travelled during the bottom two hours of the tide, keeping a close eye on the sweep if the swell is running. Park high on the dunes.

Ocean Beach is fairly shallow and has a few gutters spread out along its length. The best areas are at the top quarter of the beach as it approaches Cape Kidnappers. The best fishing at Ocean Beach is when the low tide is around dawn, so be prepared for an early start.

Kent Fraser with a fat gurnard caught in the surf. Notice the floats on the rig, designed to keep baits away from paddle crabs.

Paddle crabs can be a pain, but they do make good bait for dogfish.

Sunrise at Ocean Beach.

Getting your cast into the fish-catching zones is also essential and surfcasters should gear up with 6 or 8 kg line, shock leaders, distance-casting rigs and break-out surf sinkers. Wading will also get you closer to the gutters where the fish lie. Use small baits of fresh pilchard or salted bonito tied on firmly with bait elastic.

Gurnard and kahawai make up the bulk of catches here and when the fish are biting, good bags are not uncommon. Paddle crabs can be a nuisance and local experts have taken to using rigs with small floats to hold the baits up off the bottom

Bare Island

Between Ocean Beach and Waimarama Beach is Bare Island. Located a short distance from shore, the island has good reef structure close in and sizeable areas of foul in the deep water nearby. Boats can be launched at Clifton ramp, which is about half an hour's run away, or at Waimarama, which is very close.

Fishing around Bare Island is a fairly straightforward affair with blue cod in residence on most of the reefy areas. Kahawai are present all year; and fishing on the seabed with baited flasher rigs works particularly well for them. Snapper can prove a little more elusive. Employing a good berley trail and floating pilchard baits will turn them on if they are in the region.

About 2 km off the ocean side of Bare Island is a wreck and area of deep foul. Fishing here will produce tarakihi, groper and the odd kingfish. Use medium-sized ledger rigs or over-sized flasher rigs baited with squid and bonito. Westerly winds and strong current conditions will find the fish most eager to feed. The state of the tide is not too vital unless the water is dirty, and in that case the incoming tide is best.

There are home stays, motels and baches for rent at Waimarama. A small general store has basic provisions.

Best baits
Bonito
Pilchard
Squid
Kahawai cut baits

Recommended fishing gear
10–15 kg boat set
5/0 suicide hooks
8/0 circle hooks
4/0 flasher rigs
8/0 flasher rigs

Heavy-duty flasher rigs with extra strong hooks are ideal for fishing at Bare Island.

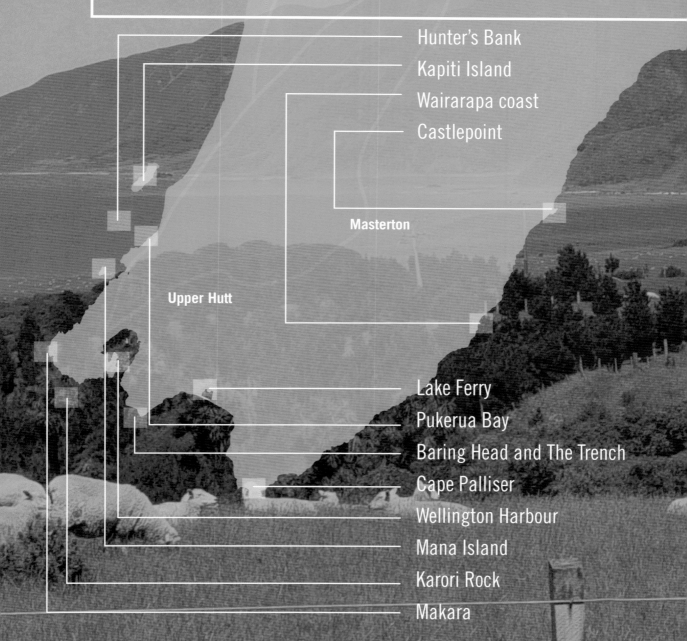

Wairarapa to Wellington

Hunter's Bank

Kapiti Island

Wairarapa coast

Castlepoint

Masterton

Upper Hutt

Lake Ferry

Pukerua Bay

Baring Head and The Trench

Cape Palliser

Wellington Harbour

Mana Island

Karori Rock

Makara

The Wairarapa Coast down to Wellington has some excellent fishing and is served by arterial roads that branch off State Highway 2. Both beach and boat fishing are available in these outlying areas.

Boat launching can be tricky with only beaches available to launch from in many areas and tractors and special beach-launching trailers are essential.

The weather can strangle fishing opportunities on this exposed coast, as the wind can be a real problem. But on those days when the weather is kind, the fishing is very rewarding.

Castlepoint and the Wairarapa coast

Castlepoint is one of the most awesome sights along the Wairarapa coast. A small natural harbour lies behind a break in a high rock wall that stretches 160 m skyward. In the uplifted reef structure, surrounded by golden sand, fossilised sea life is clearly visible in the sandstone.

A motor camp is situated at the northern end of the beach. It has cabins, powered and non-powered sites, ablution and kitchen facilities and a TV/games room. Castlepoint store and tea-rooms are on the beach front. Public toilets are located at the road end and opposite the store. Caution: the area known as 'The Reef' is extremely dangerous and sea conditions are unpredictable.

Castlepoint is located on the east coast about an hour's drive from Masterton. Turn right into Te Ore Ore Road on the northern outskirts of Masterton. This road becomes the Masterton-Castlepoint Road and leads directly to Castlepoint.

Castlepoint is a great base from which to fish the Wairarapa coast. Boats can be launched in the sheltered lagoon by most 4WD vehicles. Once out through the entrance, reefs and pinnacles are plentiful and the continental shelf is just 14 km offshore.

Wairarapa boat fishing involves anchoring on a likely pinnacle or reef and fishing with two-hook dropper rigs or baited flasher rigs. Blue cod, gurnard and kahawai are the main catches. Once you start fishing in over 50 m of water, blue cod, tarakihi and groper become more abundant.

Kingfish, sharks and albacore are also found around schools of baitfish in the deeper water; trolling with squid lures and bibbed minnows will provoke strikes.

Drift-fishing off the beaches in 20 or 30 m will find plenty of big gurnard willing to take a baited flasher rig. One problem in this region can be an overabundance of barracouta, which bite off every rig put in the water. The only cure for this problem is to move spots.

The whole of the Castlepoint area is popular with landbased anglers, with the area called 'The Reef' being the prime spot. Gurnard, kahawai, red cod, skate, kingfish and blue cod are some of the many species that are landed here. The odd hapuku caught from the shore is also reported. A long-handled gaff and strong rod are required to lift hooked fish up the rock walls.

A variety of rigs work shore-fishing off Castlepoint. A ledger rig is most popular for bottom fish and live and dead baits suspended under a float work well on kahawai and kingfish.

Being such an exposed part of the coast, any strong winds will make fishing hard, especially if they have any east in them. Weather conditions vary dramatically up and down the coast, so pay attention to local forecasts.

Best baits
Bonito
Pilchard
Squid
Kahawai cut baits

Recommended fishing gear
10–15 kg boat set
5/0 suicide hooks
8/0 circle hooks
4/0 flasher rigs
8/0 flasher rigs

Polystyrene floats are good for fishing over really snaggy ground or for livebaiting with small baits.

Castlepoint reef and lagoon – not a good day for fishing.
Photo: Chris Robinson.

Cape Palliser

To get to Cape Palliser, the southernmost tip of the North Island, by road follow State Highway 2 to Carterton and then head to Martinborough. Follow the signposts to Lake Ferry. From Lake Ferry the road follows the coast past Ngawi to Cape Palliser.

By sea, most boats come from Seaview in Wellington Harbour, where the facilities are very good, or else they're launched at Ngawi. Launching at Ngawi is a bit rugged, but the local boat club are very accommodating and on most weekends they have a large tractor operating a boat launching service and will happily launch and retrieve boats for a small donation.

A fishing rule of thumb for this area is: if the wind is from the south, don't bother. Even a light southerly will lift the swell and make conditions very unpleasant for both shorebased and boat fishermen. Because southerlies are common, on the days when conditions are right the fishing is some of the best in the Wellington region.

Finding a spot is not hard, as good reef structure is dotted all along this piece of coastline. Straight off Ngawi, Black Rocks and off the Cape Palliser lighthouse are common areas to fish. Southern species of fish are plentiful and the main targets are blue cod, tarakihi, groper and trumpeter.

The best depth to fish is the 30–60 m range. The deeper water tends to produce more groper and tarakihi. Larger flasher rigs from 4/0 to 8/0 sizes baited with squid are the best. Rods and reels should be spooled with 15–24 kg superbraid line and sinkers up to 500 g should be carried to help counter strong currents. Boat fishing is good any time you can fish here, with the top and bottom of the tide being the best times.

The road that runs from Lake Ferry to Cape Palliser follows the eastern side of Palliser Bay, and while much of the area is quite snaggy, clearer shingle beaches are good for surfcasting. Don't be put off if the water is dirty, as it can often be – the fish aren't.

During the day kahawai and red cod are common catches. The prime targets here are spotted dogfish and blue moki. To target these two species, fish with small, strong hooks baited with crayfish tail, mussel and crab baits. Tie baits firmly with bait elastic as pickers and crabs can be a real problem. Fishing at dusk and after dark are the most productive, especially when the wind is from the north. Take plenty of warm clothes as it can get chilly here, even in summer.

Ngawi has limited accommodation and bookings are essential in holiday seasons. It is possible to snorkel for crayfish and paua in very shallow water on this coast.

Best baits
Squid
Pilchard
Bonito
Mussel
Crayfish tail
Crab
Tuatua

Recommended fishing gear
Surfcasting set
10–15 kg boat set
5/0 suicide hooks
8/0 circle hooks
4/0 flasher rigs
8/0 flasher rigs
Sinkers up to 500 g
Bait elastic
Break-out sinkers

Lake Ferry

In the middle of Palliser Bay, just behind the beach, lies Lake Onoke, commonly called Lake Ferry. This shallow estuarine lake system is the outflow for the much larger Lake Wairarapa and offers many good spots and fishing options for surfcasters. The whitebaiting is also very good in season.

There is a good camping ground and caravan park on the shores of the lake, and the Lake Ferry Hotel offers accommodation and meals.

The Wellington side of Lake Ferry and Ocean Beach can be accessed from Wharekauhau via Western Lakes Rd from Featherston. A long sand and shingle spit can be driven along in 4WD vehicles all the way to the mouth of Lake Ferry. The spit is the prime area for fishing.

Fishing into the lake will produce red cod and kahawai. The more desirable fish are caught at the mouth, along Ocean Beach and off the spit.

The best conditions are when the wind is from the north, but the area is fishable in any wind not from the south. The water at the mouth of Lake Ferry is often quite murky – this has no adverse effect on the fishing.

I have seen photos of the old days when fishermen lined up with their catches of cod and kahawai. They also caught groper straight off

Lake Ferry has good accommodation, but bookings are essential in holiday seasons.

Best baits
Squid
Pilchard
Bonito
Mussel
Crayfish tail
Crab
Paua gut

Recommended fishing gear
2x surfcasting set
5/0 suicide hooks
20 kg trace line
Pulley rigs
3/0 circle hooks
4/0 flasher rigs
Bait elastic
Break-out sinkers

Spotted dogfish love to eat crabs.

the beach in this area. Unfortunately this does not happen anymore, but Lake Ferry does produce the odd surprise still. Each year a few salmon are caught near the mouth and the occasional snapper turns up amongst the common catches of kahawai, red cod, skate, blue moki and spotted dogfish.

The best approach to fishing this area is to use two surf rods set with different baits. This way all options are covered for the species that are caught here. Fish one with bonito or pilchard and the other with crayfish tail or paua gut, one of the secret and very successful baits for this area. Rig with a two-hook ledger rig and break-out sinker, or use a pulley rig with a keeper hook for greater distance.

Fishing is good all year at Lake Ferry, but spring and summer are best. The prime fishing time is during a rising tide at change of light. Dusk and after dark are best for spotted dogfish and blue moki, which feed just behind the breakers when there is a good offshore breeze.

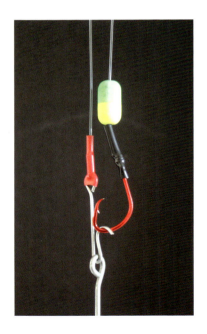

Bait clips hold the hook and bait in place, streamlining the rig and preventing the bait from ripping off.

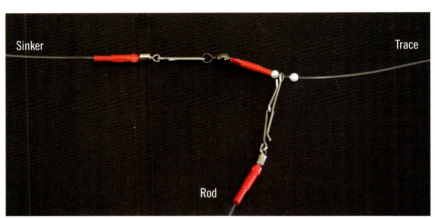

The pulley rig is set using swivels and beads. While it looks complicated it is very good for distance casting and avoiding tangles.

Baring Head and The Trench 🎣

Just around the corner from Wellington Harbour an area of foul lies in 40–60 m of water between Baring Head and Turakirae Head. Drift-fishing in this area with baited flasher rigs will produce big tarakihi and blue cod most of the year. In spring, warehou will start schooling in mid-water. Fishing under the birds with jigs and flasher rigs is the best way to target these tasty, hard-fighting fish.

Boats can be launched at any of the ramps in Wellington Harbour. Pay close attention to the weather forecast and abandon trips quickly at the first sign of weather changes.

Squid and octopus are the best baits to use in this region.

Ideal conditions are when winds are light from the northwest. Watch the weather here, as it can get up really quickly from the south. The state of the tide is not really important.

A further 5 km off Baring Head is the area known as The Trench. There are a few trenches: the main ones are Cook Strait Trench and the Nicholson Trench. These spots are clearly marked on charts and can be found with the aid of a GPS.

The Trench holds a wide variety of deepwater species, including hapuku, bass, bluenose and ling. Trips should always be limited to when the weather is good and the swell is low. The waters of Cook Strait are notorious for strong currents and changeable conditions.

The water fished varies from 130 to 220 m, so rods and reels must have suitable capacity to fish in these depths. The best rig is a 24 kg stand-up rig spooled with a minimum of 600 m

Bluenose is fairly common in the deep water off Wellington.
Photo: Cecil Alexander.

Best baits

Squid

Octopus

Barracouta

Small, just legal-size tarakihi

Recommended
fishing gear

10–15 kg boat set

24 kg stand-up set

37 kg superbraid

5/0 circle hooks

11/0 circle hooks

4/0 flasher rigs

8/0 flasher rigs

500–1000 g 'puka leads

of 37 kg superbraid. Heavy-duty dropper rigs with up to four large circle hooks, light sticks taped to the trace and 1 kg sinkers are used.

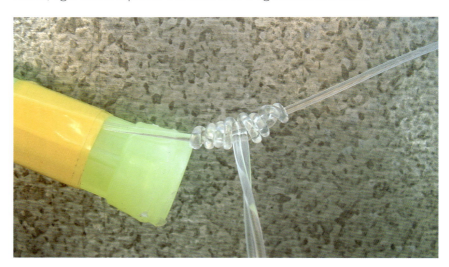

A heavy-duty dropper rig with a light stick taped to the trace.

Bait cocktails of strips of barracouta and pieces of squid should be used, as even in these depths pickers can be a problem. Small tarakihi livebaits are very good for catching big hapuku and bass.

Setting the angle of drift for the boat is critical for success in The Trench. Baits want to be near the bottom on the edge, off one of the drop-offs. Top and bottom of the tide are best as the slack current allows bait to stay longer in the strike zone.

Wellington Harbour

Fishing Wellington can be interesting... and frustrating. The strong winds that the area is famous for can often make conditions unsuitable for the better spots and daytime bait stealers can plague anglers. But at times, when the conditions are right, Wellington Harbour can produce fishing to rival any spot in the country.

Boaties should look towards the heads for the better fishing spots. The area from Eastbourne to Pencarrow Head has quite a lot of structure and during summer snapper and gurnard can be caught by berleying up in the reefy areas and fishing with pieces of pilchard and bonito. Move out a little deeper and gurnard and kahawai will be caught.

One of the most popular and productive spots is called the Falcon Shoals. The area around the Falcon Shoals is fairly shallow and in the best spot the depth is about 5 m. To locate the shoals, run between half to one kilometre south of Ward Island towards the heads. The predominant species are gurnard and kahawai, with snapper showing up in season.

Another interesting and tasty fish caught here is the elephantfish. Usually entering the harbour in spring, this unusual looking member of the shark family grubs along the bottom with its trunk-like mouth, eating crustaceans. Elephantfish give a good account of themselves on medium tackle and are very good eating.

The best way to fish the Falcon Shoals is with berley weighted to sit on the bottom. Use both 3/0 flasher rigs and running rigs set on light-action rods. The reason for this is to target the different species available. Use a 5/0 hook on the running rig, baited with half a pilchard or baby squid. On the flasher rig use salted bonito and squid.

Baits should be cast well away from the boat and it's important to let fish run before striking. The fishing can be good when it is a little choppy, mainly when wind and tide are in the same direction.

The other type of boat fishing in Wellington Harbour is targeting kahawai that enter the harbour chasing pilchards at certain times. It is easy to know when they are running because schools are clearly indicated by the small white terns that circle above the work-ups. These kahawai

Boats can be launched at any of the ramps in Wellington Harbour.

Best baits
Squid
Spotty head
Pilchard
Salted bonito

Recommended fishing gear

6–8 kg boat set
4 m surfcaster
3 m rock and wharf rod
15 kg trace
3/0 circle hooks
3/0 suicide hooks
3/0 flasher rigs
60 g chrome lures

schools can be found all around the harbour. The best approach is to drift into the schools from the upwind side, casting small silver jigs and retrieving quickly.

Surfcasting is very popular in Wellington Harbour and the locals are very in tune with what is happening. Certain species are targeted at different times of the year in different parts of the harbour.

During winter, the fishing can be tough with red cod, kahawai and barracouta being hard-earned. This can change very quickly when there is a run of baitfish. At these times kahawai fishing around the wharves in Lambton Harbour can be nothing short of spectacular. Every keen fisho in the neighbourhood will be spinning up hard-fighting kahawai for the smoker.

When the harbour starts to warm up, gurnard and then snapper start to get caught along Oriental Bay. Most of the fishing is done at the change of light and after dark and tide does not seem to play a big part in the feeding habits of the fish. The standard rig for surfcasting in Wellington Harbour is a ledger rig with two 3/0 suicide hooks baited with bonito or squid and bound with bait elastic. A spotty head is popular bait for snapper, as it is tough and can put up with pickers. Tarakihi, elephantfish, warehou and kingfish all enter the harbour at times and recently trevally and John dory have been a lot more common.

Spot selection is often governed by the wind, with the wharves and points all popular. In many cases you will be fishing right off the footpath next to where you have parked, and access to many of the other spots is also easy.

It's hard to go past a baited flasher rig.

Karori Rock

Marked by Karori Light, Karori Rock is situated west of Sinclair Head as you leave Wellington Harbour. The waters off Karori Rock can get pretty wild, with very strong currents. Trips should only be undertaken in good conditions with light winds and moderate tidal flow.

Fishing in the middle depths of 40–60 m, blue cod and tarakihi are prolific and generally of good size. To target these fish use a 4/0 flasher rig baited with squid or a ledger rig with 5/0 long-shank hooks. Carry a good selection of sinkers to cope with the effects of the changing currents.

Move out a little deeper where the structure is in 80–120 m and groper and trumpeter will be caught. Fish with a heavier tackle than closer in. Use a heavy-duty ledger rig or extra-large flasher rig baited with squid or bonito.

Drift-fishing on these spots works well, but if conditions allow, anchoring with a reef anchor is preferable.

Caution: check your chart for the no-anchor zone to the west of the Karori Rock. This is a spot for 6 m plus boats. Launching is from Wellington Harbour or around on the west coast at Makara.

Best baits
Squid
Bonito

Recommended fishing gear
10/15 kg boat set
15/24 kg boat set
5/0 long-shank hooks
4/0 flasher rigs
8/0 flasher rigs
200–1000 g sinkers

Heavy-duty droppers are good in high current areas.

Makara

Eighteen km west of Wellington, Makara offers a few shore fishing options for those who don't mind a bit of a hike. The main spot is Boom Rock. Deep water close to shore has earned 'Boom' a reputation as one of the best landbased spots in the region. It's a walk of about an hour from Makara.

Boats can be launched at Paremata, which is just off State Highway 1, thirty minutes north of Wellington in the sheltered waters of Porirua Harbour.

Best baits
Squid
Bonito
Pilchard

Recommended fishing gear
10/15 kg boat set
15/24 kg boat set
5/0 long-shank hooks
4/0 flasher rigs
8/0 flasher rigs
200–1000 g sinkers

During summer, kingfish and trevally are caught here, and because of the depth of the water, it is not unusual to catch tarakihi and warehou off this ledge.

Boat fishing around Makara is done in two main areas: in-close in water depths of 20–50 m, where tarakihi, blue cod, snapper and trevally are the main species; and out in 100–130 m, where any structure or reef supports healthy numbers of blue cod, groper and trumpeter.

The techniques for fishing the Makara coast are similar to the rest of the Wellington region, with baited flasher rigs and ledger rigs being popular choices. There is one exception: when fishing in under 50 m of water, straylining with pilchards and using berley is very effective on snapper and trevally.

Snapper are usually at their best in February and March, while the other species are present all year.

The best weather conditions are when the winds are east to northeast with the swell under 1.5 m on a rising tide.

Big trevally put up a good fight and make great eating.
Photo: Cecil Alexander.

Mana Island

Mana is one of two islands situated off the Kapiti Coast, northwest of Wellington; the other is the much larger Kapiti Island. Mana is popular due to its proximity to Porirua Harbour, and the good launching facilities at Plimmerton and Paremata. It also offers some shelter in southwesterly and northwesterly winds.

The best fishing areas are at the South Point and North Bluff, with the area facing towards shore in the middle of the island known as 'The Bridge' often producing well.

Choosing a spot to fish is a simple case of looking at the wind direction and fishing the spot offering the best protection. Both ends of the island will produce blue cod and tarakihi in 30–50 m of water.

The Bridge comes up quite shallow. Anchoring in around 10 m is the go for snapper, kingfish and John dory during summer months.

Fishing techniques for tarakihi involve the use of 3/0 flasher rigs baited with squid or mussel baits. Blue cod are caught using a ledger rig with long-shank, 6/0 hooks baited with squid or barracouta strips.

Target John dory and kingfish with a livebait on a single 8/0 circle hook fished ledger-style and weighted to the bottom.

Snapper and trevally respond well to a good berley trail in the shallows, taking pilchard and squid baits straylined amongst the foul around The Bridge.

There are plenty of areas to launch boats of all sizes around Plimmerton, Paremata and Titahi Bay. Some require boat club membership. Accommodation and all services, including dive shops, fuel and food stores, are all close to Plimmerton. A good spot to catch livebait is around the Plimmerton Bridge.

Best baits
Squid
Pilchard
Barracouta strips
Mussel

Recommended fishing gear
50 kg trace
10/15 kg boat set
8/10 kg strayline set
6/0 long-shank hooks
3/0 flasher rigs
8/0 circle hooks

Long-shank hooks are popular when targeting blue cod. They allow for easy removal, as cod can be ravenous feeders and swallow hooks easily.

Pukerua Bay

North of Plimmerton on State Highway 1, Pukerua Bay is popular for surfcasting and boat fishing. Generally the fishing could be described as hard to average most of the time. Then the odd trip will really surprise you.

The holiday towns of the Kapiti Coast are spread a few kilometres up the road and offer all the services. The easiest boat launching site is at Plimmerton. Beach launching off Paekakariki, Raumati or Paraparaumu requires a tractor or unhooking the trailer and manhandling it into the water, using a rope tow to retrieve boat and trailer.

Best baits

Squid
Pilchard
Kahawai fillet
Octopus tentacle
Bonito
Crab
Crayfish tail

Recommended fishing gear

10/15 kg boat set
10 kg strayline set
6/0 long-shank hooks
3/0 flasher rigs
8/0 circle hooks

The shore structure can be quite snaggy and anglers must be prepared to sacrifice a bit of gear. For the better spots, walk south to Wairaka Point. If the southerly is blowing, fish the corner of the bay that offers a little shelter.

Use rigs with a single dropper that can be set without snagging and fish spots where there is some clean ground. Large hard baits that can withstand the attention of pickers are also an advantage for fishing this area. Skinned octopus tentacle, salted bonito and fresh kahawai strips all work well. If you are hunting spotted dogfish, crabs and crayfish bound to the hook with bait elastic will be best.

While the general catches are spotted dogfish, rays, red cod and kahawai, just to keep things interesting the occasional really big snapper is caught.

Boat anglers will catch tarakihi, blue cod, trevally and snapper by anchoring over some of the plentiful foul that runs out to about 30 m deep off Wairaka Point. Putting down a weighted berley bomb and throwing handfuls of pilchard cubes or pellet berley away from the boat will attract plenty of fish. It is worth fishing with standard ledger rigs but also casting out big baits like half a bonito head or a whole fillet of kahawai on a strayline rig to tempt a big snapper. The snapper run from November onwards and when they come on, hauls of big fish are common.

In the deeper water about 2 km off Wairaka Point a reef rises up sharply from about 80 m. Drifting around here will produce good tarakihi, blue cod and the odd school groper.

The best time to fish is on a falling tide with light breezes. The wind direction plays a part in how the fish act. When the southerly blows the fish appear to be less active.

Hunter's Bank

Any spot that has a large amount of structure rising from deep water offers exciting fishing, and Hunter's Bank is no exception.

The reef rises from 60–80 m up to 16 m on the top pinnacles. Hunter's Bank is situated 12 km by sea from Pukerua Bay, halfway between Mana Island and Kapiti Island. Good navigation skills or a GPS are required to find the bank. Increased bird life can also indicate that the reef is nearby.

Large schools of kingfish cruise around the bank and can turn up all year, although the best schools are present from January through to May. Fish in these schools vary in size with plenty of big specimens.

At times, schools of kingfish chase baitfish to the surface and can be caught with poppers cast into the work-ups. The rest of the time, high-speed jigging and livebaiting are the most productive methods.

Bottom fish can be caught by drifting off the cliffs with ledger and flashers rigs. Tarakihi, blue cod and a variety of other bottom fish are common, along with warehou, trevally and snapper, which turn up occasionally.

When fishing on the deeper part of Hunter's Bank, or some of the other deeper structure that lies within a few miles, use ledger rigs and big slabs of bonito or barracouta to target big groper.

Trolling with small game lures and bibbed minnows when the warm currents push down the coast will produce albacore ranging in size from 2 to 20 kg.

The best conditions for bottom fishing Hunter's Bank are when the top of the tide is around midday. The kingfish are most active in the early morning and late afternoon on the rising tide. Groper are best targeted at slack tide.

Hunter's Bank is exposed from all directions and the area requires light winds and low swells to be fished safely.

A good chart, sounder and GPS are essential for fishing this area.

Best baits
Squid
Pilchard
Barracouta
Live tarakihi
Bonito

Recommended fishing gear
10/15 kg jig set
15/24 kg boat set
6/0 long-shank hooks
6/0 flasher rigs
12/0 circle hooks
Small game lures
Bibbed minnows
200 g jigs
Large poppers

Kapiti Island

The holiday towns of the Kapiti Coast and Waikanae offer all amenities and are about 50 km from Wellington City. All launching is done from the beaches in this area.

Lying approximately 6 km from shore, Kapiti Island is renowned for its spectacular bird life and diving. Many endangered species live on the pest-free island. The fishing is also very good around this, the largest island on New Zealand's west coast.

A good portion of Kapiti lies within a marine reserve where fishing is totally prohibited. Anglers should make themselves aware of the boundary markers of the reserve for obvious reasons.

The two main areas that produce good fishing around Kapiti are the many reefs and smaller islands on the southeastern end of the island and the northern side of the island between the marine reserve areas.

For a large part of the year tarakihi and blue cod are the most commonly caught species. These are usually found close to the reefs in 30–40 m of water and bite freely on flasher rigs baited with squid.

In summer, snapper turn up in big numbers in the Rauoterangi Channel between Kapiti and the mainland. After the initial runs, the snapper take up residence on the shallower reefs.

If good weather coincides with the major runs, the fishing is excellent in the Rauoterangi Channel and all rigs and techniques produce good fish. Drifting with pilchards on a two-hook rig is one of the best.

Mark Kitteridge poses with a snapper in prime condition.
Photo: Cecil Alexander.

Best baits
Squid
Pilchard
Bonito

**Recommended
fishing gear**
10/15 kg boat set
25 kg trace
10 kg strayline set
5/0 suicide hooks
Small squid lures
4/0 flasher rigs

Kingfish hunt all around the island's high current areas and headlands during the warmer months. Trolling with bibbed minnows is a good way to prospect likely looking spots and kahawai livebaits fished around any of the reefs will produce the big specimens.

Albacore come within 1 km of the back side of the island when the water temperatures get up to around 17°C. Trolling at 5 knots using a couple of small squid lures is the favoured technique. Often one of the lures will have a trolling weight attached to get it a little deeper.

Kapiti offers shelter in most conditions, except strong winds from the north and south, which swirl down the sides of the island. The currents can be very strong and great care should be taken when anchoring, and when the wind opposes the tide. The tide and wind in the same direction is beneficial when anchoring to fish.

Kingfish show up around Christmas time on the Kapiti Coast.

Wanganui to Port Waikato

Ngaruawahia

Raglan

Port Waikato

Marokopa

New Plymouth

Patea

Mokau

Wanganui

Cape Egmont

Hawera

Up the coast from Kapiti the terrain is all very similar, with long stretches of sandy beaches broken up by river mouths and shallow rocky foreshores. The undersea topography does have some reef structure and vast areas of sand and mud. There are good boat fishing, surfcasting, kite and kontiki spots all along this large stretch of coast. Boat access can be difficult, with beach and river bar launching being the norm.

Wanganui

A little over two hours' drive from Wellington – take State Highway 3 north from Bulls – Wanganui is a medium-sized town that has plenty of facilities for anglers.

It is situated in the South Taranaki Bight, a large bay that runs from Cape Egmont to Kapiti. The focal point of Wanganui is the Wanganui River. Boat fishing is dictated by the state of the river and its bar. Crossing the bar in good conditions is fairly straightforward. Top of the tide with an offshore wind is the best time to attempt it.

Boat fishing in the Wanganui region is not the easiest, with only limited areas of subsurface structure and no above surface landmarks. During winter many of the prime species are fairly scarce, with the exception of blue cod, groper and tarakihi. Less desirable species like red cod, spiny dogfish and barracouta are more usual. From November onwards the fishing picks up with snapper, kingfish and gurnard moving into the region.

As most of the structure off Wanganui is fairly flat, any patch of reef, foul or rise in the bottom is worth a look. Straight out from the river mouth in depths of 30–40 m is worth trying. Drift-fishing over the sand off the beaches in 20–30 m will produce gurnard, kahawai and snapper.

The best rigs for boat fishing are a 3/0 flasher baited with squid and bonito for bottom fishing, along with a lightly weighted pilchard cast well away from the boat and allowed to sink slowly. Small livebaits such as yellow-eyed mullet and mackerel fished on a ledger rig will catch many different predators, including John dory and kingfish. It is also worth trolling for kahawai and kingfish wide of the river mouths. The best sea conditions are when the wind is from the southeast with a light swell of 1 m or less.

Kai Iwi, just north of Wanganui, is popular with surf anglers and kite fishermen. 4WD vehicles can be used to access the beach and, while fishing can be tough, gurnard, kahawai, trevally and snapper can be caught.

Wanganui has a full range of services and accommodation. Boats can be launched in the river. Seek local advice as to the best conditions to launch.

Best baits
Squid
Pilchard
Bonito

Recommended fishing gear
8/10 kg boat set
25 kg trace
10 kg strayline set
5/0 suicide hooks
3/0 flasher rigs

Patea

North of Wanganui on State Highway 3 is the small settlement of Patea. The focal point of Patea is the boat ramp and the river mouth launching it provides.

Patea is a small town with basic facilities and accommodation. The boat ramp should only be used when the conditions are right. Patea is a good area to have a couple of boats fishing together for added safety.

Best baits

Kahawai
Barracouta
Squid
Pilchard

Recommended fishing gear

8/10 kg boat set
25 kg trace
6/0 circle hooks
Teardrop sinkers

The mouth is more like a chute than a river bar. When the swell is strong onshore, it creates quite large waves and should not be considered.

Patea is a good area to have a couple of boats fishing together for added safety.

The bottom fishing out of Patea can be full-on. Large schools of blue cod, tarakihi and snapper can be found over the reef structure south of the river mouth. These reefs are clearly marked on marine charts and GPS maps.

Part of the reason for the good fishing is lack of pressure from both commercial and amateur anglers, mainly because of the low number of days when conditions are suitable. It is a sort of natural conservation process.

Fishing with a basic two-hook dropper rig with 6/0 circle hooks and a teardrop sinker is all that is required off Patea. For blue cod, tough baits like strips of kahawai and barracouta are good, while tarakihi and snapper prefer squid and pilchard.

Fishing is best when a rising tide peaks at about 11 am. Look for weather patterns that offer a couple of days with offshore winds to settle the sea down and make the river mouth easy.

A prime blue cod.

New Plymouth

Port Taranaki is a manmade port with a good break wall offering shelter from the prevailing southwesterly wind. Pleasure boats of all sizes are easily launched from concrete ramps. New Plymouth is about 360 km from both Auckland and Wellington.

Just out from the port entrance the Sugar Loaf group of islands falls within a marine reserve and park. The reserve/park allows limited fishing – check the local regulations to make sure you know what fishing is permitted.

Small boat gamefishing is very popular off New Plymouth during summer because of the ease of boat launching, with no bars to navigate. Marlin, tuna and sharks come very close to shore. Add to this good bottom fishing and the spectacular views of snow-capped Mt Taranaki, and New Plymouth is an excellent destination.

One of the most popular fishing areas in New Plymouth is off the Waiwakeho River, a short distance north of the port. The depth at which fish can be found varies throughout the year and also depends on the species being targeted. In 20–30 m gurnard, kahawai and trevally are the most common, with snapper moving in around October. Further out, in 50–55 m, there is an area of foul ground. Use your chart or GPS to find the general area and then use the sounder to locate fish or good structure.

New Plymouth is a large city and has all the services and plenty of accommodation. Port Taranaki is a superb base for smaller craft wanting to fish the west coast.

Best baits
Squid
Pilchard
Bonito
Mullet

Recommended fishing gear
15 kg boat set
25 kg trace
100 kg trace
10 kg strayline set
6/0 circle hooks
4/0 flasher rigs
9/0 livebait hooks
Small tuna lures

Cecil Alexander holds a hard-fighting trevally. These fish are great sport on light tackle and the best for sashimi.
Photo: Cecil Alexander.

Fishing here will produce snapper, blue cod, tarakihi and John dory. The best conditions are when the tide is rising with a light east or nor'east wind.

This spot produces fish all year, with the peak time being the summer months. Fishing with livebaits is well worthwhile, producing kingfish on the surface and John dory on weighted baits fished deep. The best bottom fishing rig is a 4/0 flasher rig baited with squid, pilchard or bonito. Fish at anchor when conditions are calm and drift-fish when it's breezy.

Running out from Port Taranaki to a depth of about 90 m you will come across a spot called 'Tank Farm'. Nautical charts will show the area to head to. A rough way of locating this spot is to line up the LPG tanks on the hill with Seal Island and head out to the 85–90 m mark.

Tank Farm is a huge area of foul and holds fish all year round with tarakihi in winter and spring and snapper turning up from October onwards. Over the cooler months the occasional hapuku will also turn up to keep fishing interesting.

Fishing is best in light winds and the state of the tide has little relevance. Fishing on the anchor is the best way to go, so ensure that sufficient warp and chain are carried. Simple baited dropper rigs with enough weight to get to the bottom quickly are all that is needed to catch fish. Avoid shiny hooks as barracouta can be a real nuisance.

When travelling from spot to spot off New Plymouth, it is always worth trolling a small tuna lure as albacore are present for a good part of the year.

When heading south from Port Taranaki always go around Saddle Back Island if there is any kind of swell running, because waves rise up quickly between the island and the mainland where the bottom shallows, creating a boating hazard.

Between the Oakura and Tupuae Rivers the ocean floor is full of interesting structure: lava flows, boulders, large sandy areas and sloping banks of foul. The whole area produces a wide variety of species, many of which are not common elsewhere on the west coast.

The best way to approach the fishing here is by drifting. Start in close and move out in 10 m increments until you hit the fish. Watch for any sign of fish holding on structure. The bottom fishing is good right out to 60 m so there is plenty of scope to explore. The best conditions are light onshore winds and the swell below 1.5 m.

In close, the fish bite best on a rising tide in the morning using a drift rig consisting of small ball sinkers straight on top of a pair of 4/0 suicide hooks in water up to 40 m deep. In deeper water, use a ledger or flasher rig baited with squid or bonito bait.

At the time of writing there is discussion about making parts of this area a marine reserve.

It is very important to get the weight right when you're drift-fishing.

Mokau

Travelling north of New Plymouth along State Highway 3 you will come to the Mokau River just before the road heads inland through the Awakino Gorge. The Mokau is one of the last places that boats can be launched easily on this part of the west coast.

Two concrete ramps are well positioned inside the mouth of the river. Crossing the ever-changing bar is best done with local advice, as the channel is constantly shifting. If the swell is any more than a metre it can become very dangerous and should not be attempted.

There are two major fishing spots in the area around the Mokau River. To the south, off Whitecliffs, drift-fishing in 30–40 m will produce heaps of gurnard, kahawai and snapper. Fishing with baited flasher rigs works well on the gurnard, while the kahawai and snapper respond to lightly-weighted pilchards straylined down a berley trail.

North of Mokau is the Piritoki Reef. Trevally, kingfish and kahawai can all be caught fishing close to this piece of structure. Using shellfish berley and baiting 2/0 hooks with pieces of mussel and tuatua is the best technique for catching the large trevally that feed close to the reef.

Mokau is a pretty remote place and only has basic services. There is no major accommodation.

Best baits
Squid
Pilchard
Bonito
Mussel
Tuatua

Recommended fishing gear
15 kg boat set
6 kg baitcaster
25 kg trace
100 kg trace
10 kg strayline set
2/0 circle hooks
5/0 suicide hooks
4/0 flasher rigs

Much of the west coast shoreline looks the same. It pays to keep good bearings.

Marokopa

Whitebait move into the Marokopa River around September each year, and coinciding with the whitebait run, large schools of hard-fighting kahawai congregate around the mouth of the river. They will attack lures eagerly; often packs of fish can be seen chasing a lure.

If you are coming from the north, take State Highway 37 that runs off State Highway 3 at Hangatiki to get to Marokopa. There is a camping ground with a shop selling the basics.

Recommended fishing gear

8 kg salmon spinning set
40–60 g chrome jigs
25 kg trace
Small swivels

No bait required

The technique for fishing here is very simple. Cast and retrieve 40–60 g chrome jigs just below the surface. This can be done with a surf rod, or for a bit more sport, try a smaller casting rod with 6–8 kg line. Casts need only be 30 m or so to catch fish.

The whitebait and kahawai move in on the incoming tide and this is the best time to fish the inside of the river. When the tide starts to recede, kahawai sit in the current just outside the river mouth to catch whitebait caught in the outgoing flow.

Marokopa is a great place to introduce kids to the next level of fishing after wharf fishing.

Freshly smoked kahawai is very tasty.

Salmon fishing gear is ideal for Marokopa.

Raglan

Travelling west from Hamilton on State Highway 23 will lead you to Raglan Harbour. It will take about an hour towing a boat to get to this very picturesque spot. Raglan is well serviced for accommodation and amenities, and can be busy during holiday times.

Fishing options are plentiful, both in the harbour and beyond the notorious Raglan Bar at the harbour mouth. Raglan Harbour has two good boat ramps. Good-size trailer boats can be launched with ease. Anglers wanting to fish outside the heads who don't fancy negotiating the bar can travel south a little way to Manu Bay. This ramp gives direct access to the west coast and is very good providing there is no major onshore swell to contend with. Manu ramp only has a small, manmade break wall.

For surfcasters there are plenty of options in the harbour and down the coast, although some of the better spots require a bit of hiking down steep tracks.

Raglan is a well serviced holiday destination. The boat ramps are very good and suitable for all vehicles.

Best baits
Squid
Pilchard
Bonito
Mullet
Kahawai livebaits

Kids love catching sprats off the wharf.

The wharf by the boat ramp is an easy access spot that will produce kahawai, the odd trevally and gurnard. Kingfish are quite often seen chasing sprats during the summer months. The wharf is a good spot to take kids to catch sprats and piper, which can be used for fresh bait.

The best rock fishing spot is Papanui Point, 30 minutes south of Raglan on the coast road. Access to this spot does require a fair level of fitness. The best conditions to fish Papanui Point are when the wind is from the east and the swell is below 1.5 m. Good cloud cover seems to make the fishing especially good.

Snapper, kahawai and trevally can be caught all year while kingfish move into the area in late November. Casting hard baits well out on surf sinkers that can be anchored firmly works very well on snapper. Tossing half-pilchards with small ball sinkers into the wash around a berley trail will catch kahawai and trevally. Kingfish respond well to piper cast and retrieved slowly just below the surface or livebaits suspended below a party balloon.

A long gaff is a useful piece of equipment for landing bigger fish, as it is unwise to go to the water's edge to land fish.

Boat fishing in Raglan Harbour will produce a mixture of fish. The most productive spots are on the edges of the channels on the incoming tide. The current can get quite fierce on the outgoing.

Fishing with a 3/0 flasher rig or running rig baited with bonito or pilchard will work well.

Kahawai are plentiful in the North Island's west coast harbours.

By far the best fishing lies beyond the bar and, as previously mentioned, launching at Manu Bay is recommended. If you decide to cross the bar, travel with another boat and somebody who has local experience. Once over the bar the first hotspot is the Bar Reef, 5 km straight off the bar. A chart and/or GPS are very handy for finding this spot. If you get friendly with the locals, they may be happy to share the GPS co-ordinates with you. The reef sits in a depth of about 35 m and is surrounded by hard bottom structure. Fishing here can be a bit hit and miss most of the year. The best time is from October to December when the snapper move in on the west coast. Strike the reef at this time and good hauls of big snapper can be expected.

Fresh bonito and pilchard baits fished on ledger rigs and weighted strayline rigs catch fish. The larger snapper are caught well off the bottom.

Heading north from the Raglan Bar there are three areas of reef all named after their depths in fathoms. For example 'The 23', which is the furthest from Raglan – around 27 km to the north and 13 km offshore – lies in 23 fathoms. All these spots are clearly indicated on charts and have good formations that hold a variety of fish.

Fishing with a strayline rig will produce snapper, kahawai and trevally. Trolling the structure with bibbed minnows in summer will provoke strikes from kingfish. Using large kahawai livebaits trolled slowly over the structures will produce action from big kingfish and the odd shark.

Between Raglan and Kawhia Harbours is a large island called Gannet Rock. As you would expect, it is home to a large gannet colony. The trip is around 30 km from Raglan and is best when the sea is calm.

Fishing around Gannet Rock is very good, with a variety of species present most of the time. During summer, pelagic gamefish are caught very close the island.

For bottom fishing, the best option is to anchor on a piece of reef close to the island and set up a good berley trail and fish with 4/0 flasher rigs baited with pilchard and squid. It is always worth putting out a kahawai livebait because big kingfish and even the odd marlin are caught using this technique.

There are many other good spots off the Raglan coastline and on many days simply drift-fishing in 30–40 m with baited flasher rigs will produce a wide variety of species.

Recommended fishing gear

15 kg livebait set
10 kg boat set
4–m surfcaster
25 kg trace
150 kg trace
10/0 livebait hooks
5/0 suicide hooks
4/0 flasher rigs

Port Waikato

The mouth of New Zealand's longest river, the Waikato, enters the sea at Port Waikato. Popular with whitebaiters and duck hunters, the river fans out, broken up by swampy marshland, into a load of small arteries before converging into one river and entering the sea.

Port Waikato has basic shops and amenities with limited holiday accommodation. When accessing the north side of the river you have to go down forestry roads. These lead to a nice picnic area. Drag-netting for flounder and mullet can be very good. The boat ramps are suitable for all vehicles and boats up to 6 m plus.

Best baits

Pilchard
Bonito
Tuatua
Pipi

Recommended fishing gear

3–4 m surf rod
25 kg trace
Break-out sinkers
5/0 suicide hooks
4/0 flasher rigs

The sand dunes at the mouth of the Waikato River are the best spot to fish.

The best fishing is right at the mouth of the river. It can be approached from either Port Waikato, by heading west from Pokeno off State Highway 1, or via Waiuku south of Auckland. Boats can be launched on both sides of the river on decent ramps. The river has a defined channel but no navigation markers and it does shallow quickly in some areas, so care must be taken not to run aground.

Surfcasting is the ideal way to fish the mouth of the river and is just as productive as boat fishing. The best way to access it is to take a 4WD or quad-bike up to the mouth at low tide from Port Waikato.

Kahawai and trevally can be caught fairly consistently all year, but the really hot time is when the whitebait enters the river from September onwards. The fishing when this happens can be frantic.

The best time to fish is on a rising tide when there has not been a lot of rain. Rain can cause large amounts of debris to be washed up and down the river, which fouls lines and baits, making it very hard to fish.

Port Waikato is the ideal place for novice anglers as even short casts will get bites. The wind plays little part in the fishing here, as the whole area is sheltered regardless of wind direction.

It is vitally important that anglers use break-out sinkers to hold in the strong currents at the river mouth, otherwise baits will be swept back to shore. Most rigs work well when baited with small pieces of pilchard or bonito bait. Using pipi or tuatua bait will tempt trevally that school around the mouth.

You will catch the odd fish other than kahawai and trevally. Large bronze whaler sharks and kingfish come into the river to chase spawning mullet in summer. The best spot to target snapper is on the ocean side of the mouth of the river after long periods of settled weather.

Sunset beach on the ocean side of Port Waikato is good for kite and kontiki fishing when the wind is in the east. Around October this beach produces more than its share of 10 kg plus snapper.

South Island

D'Urville Island

French Pass

Nelson

Stephens Island

Trio Islands

Kenepuru and Pelorus Sounds

Motunau

Banks Peninsula

Rakaia River

Otago Region

French Pass

The top of the South Island is blessed with a fantastic maze of islands and headlands that form the harbours and coves of the Marlborough Sounds. This unique area offers boaties and fishermen an absolutely huge array of areas to explore and fish.

There is good accommodation at French Pass, but booking is advised. Check with locals as to safe boating practices when navigating French Pass.

Best baits

Pilchard
Bonito
Squid
Live mackerel

Recommended fishing gear

10/15 kg jig outfit
25 kg trace
50 kg trace
5/0 suicide hooks
4/0 flasher rigs
7/0 livebait hooks
Bibbed minnows
150–200 g speed jigs

French Pass is rated by many as one of the best fishing spots in the South Island. French Pass is located at the outer entrance of the Marlborough Sounds and separates D'Urville Island from the mainland. A good boat ramp is located at the end of French Pass Rd, which is about two hours' drive from Nelson on State Highway 6, turning off at Rai Valley.

The currents move very swiftly through the narrow gap at the Pass, causing some very impressive water disturbances which boaties should approach with caution.

Blue cod can be caught at the top and bottom of the tide before the current gets too much of a run on. During summer, kingfish hunt through French Pass. Jigging with 150–200 g jigs retrieved to the surface at high speed and trolling with bibbed minnows are both productive ways of catching these fish. When the current is not running too hard, drift-fishing with mackerel livebaits fished close to the bottom will attract strikes.

The Marlborough Sounds has a very productive snapper fishery and French Pass is one of the spots where, when the snapper are on, good catches can be expected.

High-speed jigging is deadly on schooling kingfish.

Blue cod is a much-prized eating fish in the South Island.
Photo: Daryl Crimp.

Trio Islands

A short boat trip north of French Pass a group of three islands sits in an area of the Marlborough Sounds that is quite exposed to wind and swell.

The hard bottom structure around the Trio Islands is blue cod territory, producing good-sized specimens. Kingfish hunt around the reefs that connect the islands and can be caught using livebaits, or by trolling. Move off the islands a little and tarakihi will be found in slightly deeper water.

Snapper will respond to a variety of techniques, especially when a berley trail is used. A light southwesterly coupled with a rising tide at change of light is the best time to target snapper. Fish the shallow reefs or the edge of the islands where it drops off to sand.

Trio Islands are exposed to wind and swell. Check forecasts prior to fishing there.

Best baits
Pilchard
Bonito
Squid
Live mackerel

Recommended fishing gear
10/15 kg jig outfit
25 kg trace
50 kg trace
5/0 suicide hooks
4/0 flasher rigs
7/0 livebait hooks
Bibbed minnows

Be prepared to get your arms stretched fishing around the Sounds.

D'Urville Island

The whole circumference of D'Urville Island offers attractive water to fish. Quite a few of the spots are influenced by strong currents, which can require the use of heavier sinkers and rigs to suit the conditions, and these are often hard on tackle.

To get to D'Urville Island launch at French Pass Road boat ramp.

Best baits

Kahawai
Squid
Shellfish
Tuatua

Recommended fishing gear

15 kg boat set
40 kg trace
Flasher rigs
Ledger rigs
2/0–3/0 hooks
100–300 g sinkers

Blue cod and tarakihi are the main species taken bottom fishing over reefy areas, especially at Cape Stephens on the northern end and at the Rangitoto Islands.

The southern end of D'Urville Island has a large area of exposed reef called Paddock Rocks. This is a good area to prospect when the wind is from the northeast.

Fishing techniques vary depending on the target species. Blue cod require little finesse and will bite freely on flasher rigs and ledger rigs baited with hard baits such as squid or strips of kahawai. Tarakihi require a little more stealth; use rigs with smaller hook sizes in the 2/0 to 3/0 range. Mollusc and shellfish baits are preferred by tarakihi, with tuatua proving particularly tempting to these reef fish.

Kingfish and snapper can be targeted with live and dead baits fished on running rigs. It is important to keep sinker weights adjusted to cope with the current or speed of drift.

Anchoring and drift-fishing both work well. Drifting is preferred when the winds are light and anchoring is best in the areas of strong current.

Use 2/0 flashers and shellfish baits to tempt tarakihi.
Photo: Daryl Crimp.

Stephens Island

Just to the north of D'Urville Island is Stephens Island. For anglers who enjoy the challenge of deepwater fishing, the waters just off Stephens Island offer plenty of opportunity to test their skills on hapuku and bass, species which are generically called groper in the South Island.

Weather dictates opportunities to fish these spots as they are exposed from all quarters. The ideal conditions are little swell and light winds.

To find the fish you'll need a chart plotter and a good sounder, as you will be fishing in depths of over 100 m. Look for the pinnacles that rise from the sea floor about 1.5 km north of the island or fish over areas of mixed foul 2 km to the west.

The main trick to successful groper fishing is seeing where the fish are hanging and setting your drift so that baits reach the bottom in that area. Make adjustments for changes in wind and tide. Big groper are mainly caught in winter and spring and school groper are present most of the year.

If conditions allow, it is always worth a shot drifting this area as other species like bluenose warehou and trumpeter are caught periodically.

The best rig for fishing the deeper water off Stephens Island is a sturdy rod and reel spooled with 500 m of non-stretch line. Use a two-hook dropper rig with one 6/0 and one 9/0 circle hook. This way you can hook smaller reef fish which, by struggling on the line, attract groper to the larger bait.

The daily limit for groper is three per person.   Photo: Daryl Crimp.

Stephens Island is a wildlife sanctuary and home to many rare and endangered species.

Best baits
Bonito
Squid
Live tarakihi
Fillets of kahawai

Recommended fishing gear
15/24 kg boat outfit spooled with non-stretch line
80 kg trace
6/0–9/0 circle hooks
8/0 flasher rigs

Kenepuru and Pelorus Sounds

Moving into the inner Marlborough Sounds, Kenepuru and Pelorus Sounds offer good fishing for snapper, kahawai, blue cod and kingfish.

Pelorus and Kenepuru Sounds are extremely popular holiday destinations and there is plenty of accommodation and services. During the peak of summer, the waterways carry a lot of boat traffic and this affects the fishing. The whole area is renowned for good moorings and picturesque bays.

It can be harder to find spots where the blue cod reach legal size in the inner sounds. Using circle hooks will make it easier to release small fish. One of the main features of fishing in Kenepuru Sound are the mussel farms, which are very attractive to snapper and kingfish. Another aspect of fishing this area is the vast length of coastline available to shorebased anglers.

The two main boat launching points for Kenepuru and Pelorus Sounds are at Havelock, on State Highway 6, and Portage, which is on the Kenepuru Rd. Both of these ramps are suitable for any kind of vehicle and usable at all states of the tide.

The technique for success in the Kenepuru and Pelorus Sounds relies on an ambush approach. Set up in areas where fish move, like mussel

Sunset on Pelorus Sound.

Photo: Darryl Crimp.

farms, points such as Scotts Point – or "Yncya Bay", as the locals call it – situated halfway up Pelorus Sound, and headlands that fall into channels off Portage and the island nearby. Fish with up to four rods baited with different baits. Set them at various distances from the boat and keep up a steady stream of berley.

The mussel farms are very good when workers are harvesting or setting spat, as this acts as a natural berley. Livebaits such as sprats and yellowtail set on a two-hook running rig will often tempt the biggest snapper. Pilchard, squid and strips of fresh kahawai will also tempt most other species.

The same technique applies to fishing off the shore. Use multiple rods set with different baits. Easy access spots can be found all along Kenepuru Rd. (Note: some areas require landowner permission to access.)

The time of year is critical when fishing in Kenepuru and Pelorus Sounds. Winter and spring can be a tough time to catch a decent fish. As the water temperature increases, the snapper move in and hang around until autumn. The seasonal fishing can be spectacular, with anglers catching lots of double-figure fish.

The tide also plays a major role in fish movements in this area. In general terms, fish will move into the shallows on a rising tide and drop back into areas of deeper water on the outgoing.

Kingfish are a lot more common in this part of the world than people realise. To catch them it's just a matter of using the right techniques. Small livebaits like yellowtail, small kahawai or piper (garfish) fished either on the bottom or on a float catch kingfish, as will poppers cast to fish that are hanging around the mussel farms.

As you move into the outer Pelorus Sound, blue cod and tarakihi fishing improves, especially around the Chetwodes and the northern side of Forsyth Island. Techniques and conditions are the same as those for D'Urville Island.

Best baits
Pilchard
Squid
Live sprats
Strips of kahawai

Recommended fishing gear
8/10 kg strayline outfit
4–6 kg baitcaster
20 kg trace
4/0–6/0 circle hooks

Double-figure fish are not uncommon in the Marlborough Sounds.

Nelson

Nelson is a beautiful city that offers a full range of services and accommodation. During holiday periods the population swells dramatically.

Best baits

Pilchard
Squid
Salted bonito
Live yellowtail
Pipi

West of the Marlborough Sounds, on State Highway 6, is Tasman Bay and the city of Nelson, often overlooked in favour of the Marlborough Sounds.

Nelson has a microenvironment that makes it a very interesting fishery. Snapper and kingfish are seasonal, while tarakihi, gurnard, blue cod and kahawai are present most of the time.

To fish the eastern side of Tasman Bay, travel the Rai Valley Rd, turn off and head to the ramp at Okiwi. This ramp is good from mid to high tide and suitable for most trailer boats.

The main fishing areas are around the islands at the entrance to Croisilles Harbour. Fishing is good close to the islands on the hard structure. Catches are mainly made up of blue cod and tarakihi, with the odd surprise species turning up.

Cape Soucis and the surrounding reef offer much the same as the islands, with blue cod and tarakihi making up the bulk of catches. Fish with 2/0 flasher rigs with mollusc bait when targeting tarakihi and change your bait to salted bonito to target gurnard, which are commonly caught drifting over the sand.

Around Pepin Island the points and headlands are all very productive for a wide variety of fish. The most productive depths to fish are around 15 and 20 m.

To fish for snapper in this region, techniques used are very similar to those in the North Island, as the reef structure and water depths are alike. Snapper start to move into the area in late spring-early summer and school up on the mud and sand off Delaware Bay in fairly shallow water.

Anchoring and using a good berley trail will attract these schooling fish to the boat. Standard running rigs and weighted strayline rigs work well. Weights should be chosen to suit the current. Drifting with baited flasher rigs can pay dividends, especially when the fish are first moving in and up and not holding in a particular area. This technique will also provide a bycatch of gurnard and kahawai.

Right in the heart of Nelson there are some prime fishing possies that are easy to get to and serviced by good boat ramps. Formed naturally, the Boulder Bank is a long spit that offers reasonable boat fishing on the seaward side and around the entrance. The main targets here are snapper after they have moved in from schooling over the sand. Snapper will also move into islands and foul off Croisilles Harbour at the same time and can be found until the beginning of winter.

Well-presented baits straylined down a constant berley trail will tempt snapper. Rig up with a pair of 6/0 suicide hooks tied on 20 kg trace. Cast baits well away from the boat. Use a second, lighter rig with 2/0–3/0 hooks and smaller pieces of bait to pick up a variety of other species.

In summer and autumn kingfish hunt baitfish along the entire length of the Boulder Bank. Trolling with bibbed minnows will produce the odd strike, while putting out livebaits while snapper fishing should catch kingfish more consistently.

Fishing along the Boulder Bank is good when wind and tide flow together.

Rabbit Island forms another piece of interesting structure in the Nelson district. The island offers good shelter from prevailing winds and is the ideal place for smaller craft to fish. Although the inside of Rabbit Island can be a bit of a nursery for smaller fish at times, fishing with 4–6 kg tackle will provide good action and the odd bigger fish.

Try targeting the rising tide at change of light. Set a trap on the edge of channels by setting a pilchard cube berley trail and casting pilchard baits the same size as the berley chunks with single 4/0 circle hooks concealed in the soft mouthfuls. This technique will catch snapper, kahawai and trevally.

On the ocean side of Rabbit Island the fishing is a good for surfcasters and boat fishers alike. Surfcasting is best on the bottom of the tide and the start of the incoming. Use shellfish and pilchard baits during the day and at change of light try crab or crayfish tail to catch dogfish.

Boat fishing the ocean side can be done off the anchor or while drifting. Drifting with small flasher rigs will produce plenty of gurnard and mixed bags of fish, while anchoring wide of the east and west entrances on an incoming tide will produce more snapper.

Recommended fishing gear

8/10 kg strayline outfit
4–6 kg baitcaster
2/0–4/0 flasher rigs
20 kg trace
50 kg trace
7/0 livebait hooks
6/0 suicide hooks
4/0 circle hooks

Daryl Crimp with a nice South Island red.
Photo: Daryl Crimp.

Motunau

Motunau is a small settlement with basic facilities and accommodation.

Best baits
Pilchard
Squid
Bonito

Recommended fishing gear
15 kg boat set
4/0 flasher rigs
40 kg trace
6/0–9/0 long shank hooks
6/0 circle hooks
Small tuna lures
Bibbed minnows

As you travel down the East Coast on State Highway 1 the continental shelf comes close to shore at Kaikoura, an area famous for whale and dolphin watching.

The reason for the abundant seabird and mammal life is the concentration of plankton and krill caused by upwelling currents hitting the continental shelf. The area is largely devoid of islands or headlands, so fish are found in areas where the bottom rises or falls suddenly, or where there are areas of subsurface structure.

As you head south the Motunau turnoff is marked at Greta Valley. Motunau is a small settlement close to the mouth of the Motunau River and beach. Care should be taken when attempting the tricky river bar. Local knowledge is a must, as is clement weather and the right tide.

The main structure for anglers is Motunau Island and the reef close to it. The favoured fishing spot is a reef in 20–30 m of water on the eastern side of the island. An easy way to locate the right spot is to fish near the crayfish pot buoys set close to the reef.

In this part of the country, when conditions are good enough to get out, the fishing is normally ON and berley is not necessary. Blue cod are always eager to take just about any offering that is sent to the bottom.

There is plenty of flounder in the estuary.

The favoured rig is a heavy, two- or three-hook dropper with extra-long-shank 6/0-8/0 hooks. The reason for the extra-long shanks is to allow for easy removal of blue cod as they swallow baits deeply. Circle hooks prevent deep hooking, but it can take a little longer to unhook the fish.

Another species that becomes more common as you head south is the trumpeter, a hard-fighting reef fish that grows in excess of 15 kg. To increase your chances of catching trumpeter, try using squid bait.

The best and probably only condition to consider fishing Motunau is when the wind is light and from a northeasterly direction. As previously mentioned, the fish are normally free-feeding off Motunau – the local's reckon that either side of the high tide is best, but this may be due to suitable bar crossing times rather than bites.

The fishing is fairly consistent year-round with the odd different species turning up over summer. Albacore can be targeted fairly consistently by trolling small tuna lures and bibbed minnows during the warmer months.

Small strong circle hooks are good when cod and tarakihi are around as they prevent the cod from swallowing the hook.

Alain Jorion with a huge trumpeter.
Photo: John Eichelsheim.

Banks Peninsula

Banks Peninsula has good boat ramps to access the harbours and is close to most facilities.

Best baits
Pilchard
Squid
Bonito
Live kahawai

Recommended fishing gear
10 kg boat outfit
4/0 flasher rigs
20 kg trace
7/0 livebait hooks
6/0 long-shank hooks
4/0 circle hooks

Banks Peninsula punctuates the area between Christchurch and Ashburton and has two harbours: Lyttelton on the northern side and Akaroa on the eastern end. Both can be used to gain access to good sea fishing in the many bays and headlands around the Peninsula.

Godley Head is a rocky outcrop on the left-hand heads of Lyttelton Harbour. The area has plenty of reef and large areas of kelp that shelter blue and red cod, kahawai and trumpeter.

The best of the fishing is in 30 m of water over the top of the tide. In late summer it is not unusual to find kingfish hanging around Godley Head. These fish can be targeted with livebaits or by trolling bibbed minnows around the edge of the drop-off. The best rig for bottom fishing is a ledger rig baited with bonito or squid.

The channel at Akaroa Head at the mouth of Akaroa Harbour is a good spot during summer. Blue cod and kahawai can be caught in a wide area in depth of 30–40 m. Flashers and ledger rigs work equally well. Fish with baits like pilchard and bonito.

Fishing is best over the top of the tide as the current can get really strong on the outgoing tide. Keep an eye out for southerly winds that create a big chop very quickly.

Red cod are pretty common in South Island harbours.   Photo: Daryl Crimp.

Big, fat kahawai offer good sport.
Photo: Daryl Crimp.

Rakaia River

As you head south from Christchurch along State Highway 1 you will come to the Rakaia River. It is renowned for runs of salmon returning to the Rakaia in mid-November to start their migration to their spawning grounds in the river's headwater tributaries.

The main salmon fishing season runs from January to mid-April, but it can be affected dramatically by weather. The best time to plan a trip to fish for salmon is during February and March. The best fishing is after a **fresh**. This is when the river levels rise after rain.

The type of salmon we have in New Zealand is the Quinnat or Chinook, which grows up to 20 kg in this country.

Salmon fishing techniques for New Zealand salmon rivers are quite straightforward, but there are some basic skills you need for success. Salmon lie hard on the bottom of the river, so you must have your lure close to the bottom to be successful. Feeling the lure bang off the rocks on the bottom is a good indication that the lure weight and retrieve speed are right.

The Rakaia is situated close to plenty of amenities. Good fishing guides operate jet boat salmon fishing adventures. There are special regulations for salmon fishing. A licence is required and can be obtained from local fishing tackle stores.

Shoulder to shoulder fishing can prove tense when you hook up at the Rakaia River.
Photo: Malcolm Bell.

Recommended fishing gear

4 m surf set

2.5 m heavy spin set

40–90 g Zed spinners

Spoon lures

Keel weights (where legal)

Good swivels

Waders

No bait required

A nice Rakaia salmon.

Photo: Malcolm Bell.

Salmon stay close to channels and will lie in the deeper parts of pools. To work pools thoroughly, start at the head of the pool and work your way down. Fan-cast at different angles to the bank to work different pockets of water. Start at 90 degrees to the bank or even a little upstream to give the lure a good chance of reaching the bottom quickly and covering the most water.

As salmon stop feeding once they enter the river, strikes usually come from aggression as lures are pulled through the fish's territory. Persevering in spots that are holding fish will often pay dividends.

At the mouth of the Rakaia fishing is often shoulder to shoulder when the fish are running. The most successful anglers are those who cast furthest. They tend to use surf rods with fixed or free-spool reels spooled with 8–15 kg line. Non-stretch braid lines have been gaining popularity with salmon anglers recently, due to their fine diameter and positive hook-ups. Gear should cast lures up to around 150 g.

As fish move up the river, gear can be scaled down as casting distance is not as critical and rods of 2.5–3 m with lighter line and smaller, lighter lures are quite practical.

Lure choice is a personal thing – spoons and zed-spinners in a variety of sizes and colours will work. Bright orange and yellow colours work well when the water is discoloured and plain chrome is number one most other times. Small, good quality swivels are essential to avoid line twist caused by spinning lures.

Otago Region

Travelling south there are many other rivers that are good for salmon fishing, such as the Rangitata and Waitaki, and vast areas of coast to explore.

The main city of Dunedin is serviced by Otago Harbour, known for the salmon run that still occurs, but not with the same volume of fish as in the past.

The favoured techniques are to use live and dead baits suspended below polystyrene floats fished off the local wharves, or trolling silver spoons on paravanes and downriggers from boats at the entrance to the harbour.

The Otago region

Weather conditions during winter can severely limit fishing opportunities in this region. The weather from January through to May are more reliable.

10 kg plus trumpeter.

Photo: John Eichelsheim.

Best baits
Squid
Bonito
Barracouta
Kahawai

Recommended fishing gear
10–15 kg boat set
6/0 long-shank hooks
6/0 circle hooks
40 kg trace

Outside the harbour, fish numbers and average size are good but the number of species available is greatly reduced this far south. Blue cod, groper and trumpeter are the most common and sought after.

Karitane is to the north of Dunedin. The ocean side of the point formed by the Waikouaiti River, about 1 km out, has kelp forests in 20–25 m of water. Fishing on the outside edge of the kelp will produce blue cod and trumpeter in good numbers as the tide rises.

Tackle needs to be beefy to winch fish that get into the kelp. Dropper rigs tied with short loops and 6/0 circle hooks are the go. Squid will work well as bait, along with firmer baits of kahawai and barracouta.

Out from Sandfly Bay, on the ocean side of the Otago Peninsula, is Tow Rock. Clearly marked on charts, this large, exposed rock produces good fishing over summer. As with Karitane, the best area to anchor is on the edge of the kelp in 30–40 m of water so that the boat hangs back towards the rock.

Any winds from the south knock out this spot, whereas light north or northwesterly winds are good. Standard dropper rigs will work fine when the fish are on the bite and 4/0 flasher rigs can improve fishing when the fish are slow to bite. Launching is possible at a number of spots around the coast. Check with locals for the best options.

The area from Brighton down to Taieri is good for drift-fishing as there are areas of low reef that hold good blue cod. A little further offshore groper move onto the low foul in spring.

Taieri Mouth is a picturesque seaside fishing village located at the mouth of the Taieri River on the east coast of the South Island. It is an easy 30-minute drive from Dunedin. Taieri Beach is sheltered from the force of the sea by a reef running parallel to the beach. A boat ramp is also available (seek local advice before leaving as the sandbar is difficult to negotiate).

Bait presentation

Why have I made special mention of bait presentation at the end of the book? Well, the answer is quite simple. In the introduction I covered the basics of looking for a spot and choosing the right techniques to fish it. All this information could be wasted if a simple step like presenting a bait so that it stays on the hook and looks appetising to the fish is neglected.

Many times I have been out on boats where some anglers are missing out during a hot bite. Some are just unlucky, but many others are just not taking the time to present their bait in a manner that is likely to catch them fish.

So the message is, pay attention to details. It's nothing new: sharp hooks, good knots and good bait presentation will catch you more fish!

This is how not to bait up!

Tying off with a half-hitch will stop baits being easily ripped off.

Flashers only need to be tipped with bait.

Pay close attention to hook placement.

Baits for surfcasting should be tied on with bait thread to prevent them flying off when casting and to stand up to pickers and crabs.

Make sure baits lie straight and look natural – unlike in this photo!

The last bait

As an angler I have a reputation for always having one more bait and being the last to wind in my line, usually as the motor is started at the conclusion of a fishing trip. This, I believe, stems from a dogged determination. The reason is not to catch the last fish, as many have thought! Rather, it's my way to make the enjoyment I derive from fishing last as long as possible.

From the beginning, this book was never going to be a complete guide. I'm sure I will be criticised by anglers more knowledgeable than me about fishing in certain areas, or for neglecting some areas altogether. I acknowledge any such failings and look forward to learning more about this great pastime I so love – perhaps with the assistance of those same people.

However, in a small way, I hope this book will encourage more people to take up the sport of fishing so that, as conservationists and anglers, we will have a stronger collective voice to lobby effectively for sustainable fishing stocks – the future for both recreational and commercial fishers.

In the initial acknowledgements I thanked all anglers who provided me with information that found its way into this book. It would be remiss of me not to mention a few special people I rate as my fishing buddies:

Bong Wong, who took me on surfcasting missions when I was young at a time when my life could have gone in any direction.

Richard Baker, whom I have known since my school days and who literally dragged me all round the country as we discovered for ourselves many of the spots in this book.

Craig Worthington, whose no-nonsense approach and laid-back fishing style is coupled with a wealth of knowledge about the biology of fish – I gained plenty from him.

Gary Kemsley is an angler who can catch fish in a puddle. A lifetime's worth of learning has gone into knowing how to make a spot fire, and this is a unique skill which I value greatly.

John Eichelsheim and Mark Kitteridge, with their absolute commitment to fishing, have given me the advantage of shortcutting what for many is a learning curve that can not be completed in a lifetime.

Kent Fraser, aka Monkey, with whom I always seem to end up on an adventure, even on the most ordinary of fishing trips. Just by trying different things with Kent, I learnt so much.

Not surprisingly, these guys I fish with are also some of my closest friends!

Glossary

bait – animal or vegetable material used to bait a hook to catch fish. Today, sometimes also means artificial materials, like flavoured soft plastics, formulated to catch fish.

baitcaster – small, overhead reels able to cast relatively light baits and lures. Designed primarily for freshwater fishing, some of the more robust models are popular with light tackle sea fishers. Baitcasters require a reasonable amount of skill to cast successfully.

baitfish – any fish, usually small, preyed upon by other fish. Baitfish are often useful to the angler as a bait source.

beach spike – a spike or stand, usually metal, sometimes plastic, thrust into the sand to support a surfcasting rod.

berley – minced, ground or chopped fish, shellfish and other material used to attract fish closer to the angler. Berley is often sold ready-made as frozen blocks or dried pellets. It can be dispensed at the surface or anywhere in the water column via a mesh bag or weighted cage. See also 'chum' and 'groundbait.'

bibbed minnow – a naturalistic, fish-shaped trolling and casting lure of plastic or wood equipped with an angled plastic or metal bib to make it wobble seductively when drawn through the water.

bonito – a small, tropical tuna not normally present in our waters. The name 'bonito', is commonly used to describe locally caught skipjack tuna, particularly when it is sold as bait.

bottom fish – fish that spend most of their time at or near the seabed. Many popular sportfish are predominantly bottom fish: tarakihi, snapper, blue cod, hapuku/groper, etc.

bottom fishing – fishing near the bottom of the sea for bottom fish like tarakihi, blue cod or snapper.

break-out sinkers – streamlined casting sinkers with wire tines that hold the bottom. The tines either bend or snap free of special grooves moulded in the lead when sufficient pressure is applied, breaking the tines out of the bottom.

breakwater – a manmade structure, usually of rock or masonry, designed to shelter harbours, river bars, boat ramps, etc. from the worst effects of wind and sea. Also called seawall and breakwall.

bycatch – fish taken 'by mistake' when targeting other species. They are often a welcome addition to the day's bag.

cast weight – the amount of weight a rod is designed to cast. Most surf rods have a cast weight range in ounces or grams printed near the foregrip.

chemically sharpened (hooks) – hooks whose points have been dipped in a chemical bath to ensure a needle-sharp point. Most of the better hooks on the market are chemically sharpened and require no honing out of the box.

chum – another name for berley; usually fish pieces chopped, minced or ground into fine particles to attract fish.

circle hook – a hook with a recurved point, sometimes nearly touching the shank, popular for bottom fishing and for use with dropper rigs.

double-figure – refers to fish weight in pounds or kilos but you need to know which! A snapper of 10 kg or more is a double-figure fish, but for someone working in pounds 10 lb fish is double-figure.

downrigger – a heavy weight on a cable and drum system used to troll a lure or bait deep down in the water column. The lure is attached to the downrigger by a quick-release clip that releases the line when a fish strikes, allowing the angler to play the fish from the rod.

drogue – a parachute-like device dragged from the side, transom or bow of a boat to slow its drift in windy conditions.

dropper (rig) – a rig with one or more short branches projecting from the main line or 'trunk'. Hooks are tied to each of the branches and a sinker is tied to the bottom of the mainline or trunk. See also 'flasher' and 'ledger'.

eggbeater – another name for a threadline, fixed spool, open-face or spinning reel.

fixed spool reel – spinning reel where the rotor and bail arm revolves around a vertical spool. Also called eggbeater, open face and threadline reels.

flasher (rig) – dropper rigs with one or more attractor flies tied into the hooks. Attractor material can be coloured fabric, nylon, metal foil, flashy synthetic or natural feather. See also sabiki.

fresh – a flood or rush of freshwater down a river and into an estuary after heavy rain.

groundbait – small pieces of bait fed into the water to attract fish to the hook bait. See berley and chum.

gauge – a measure of wire thickness. The higher the number, the thinner the wire. Hooks are made from wire and their thickness is expressed as a gauge number.

inshore – close to shore (see offshore).

jig – a fish-shaped metal lure designed for casting and retrieving across the surface or for dropping to the bottom and retrieving vertical with the rod imparting extra action. Jigs are not normally suitable for trolling.

jigging – fishing a jig vertically through the water column.

landbased (fishing, fisher) – fishing from the land/shore rather than out of a boat.

ledger rig – a rig with the sinker at the bottom and one or more hooks on branches off the main line. Also called dropper rig. The most popular and versatile rig for a variety of fishing situations.

lightstick – plastic tube available in various sizes and colours containing a luminous chemical. A chemical reaction is initiated by bending the lightstick to break a capsule containing the catalyst. Lightsticks typically glow for 10–12 hours. Lightsticks are useful for deepwater fishing and nightfishing for gamefish like broadbill.

livebait – a fish or other animal used alive as bait to attract larger fish to the hook.

monofilament – line made from a single unbroken chain of molecules. Commonly called nylon.

onshore (wind) – a wind blowing off the ocean onto the shore (see offshore).

offshore – away from shore, i.e., offshore islands.

offshore (wind) – a wind blowing off the shore and out to sea.

pelagic (fish) – fish that live in the upper layer of the sea. These surface feeders include the fastest and most sought after sportfish. Typical pelagic species in New Zealand include all the tunas, billfish (marlin, shortbill spearfish), slimy mackerel, kahawai and kingfish (sometimes).

pilchard – small, herring-like baitfish with oily flesh. Closely related to the sardine, pilchards are sold fresh and frozen for use as fish bait. 'Pilchards' – some of the imported baits are different species – are sourced from all over the world for bait in New Zealand, but the best bait is our own locally caught pilchard, *Sardinops pilchardus*.

polymer – a string of molecules. Common polymers include nylon and fluorocarbon. Most nylon fishing line includes more than one polymer, often incorporating a harder outer material and a softer, more pliable core.

popper – a casting lure that creates a lot of surface commotion when worked by the angler using the rod. Poppers imitate frantically fleeing baitfish and attract strikes from large surface predators like kingfish.

recurve(d) hooks – see 'circle hooks'.

sabiki – usually small many-branched flasher-type rigs designed to take small baitfish. Flies can consist of latex, fish skin, metal foil or feather. They are similar to flasher rigs but generally smaller, constructed from lighter material and with more branches on each 'string' – up to 12.

shock leader – a length of heavy nylon or fluorocarbon, stronger than the main line, designed to take the shock of casting. Shock leaders allow full power casts that would snap the main line.

skipjack – a small tuna, found locally in summer months, popular as bait. Often erroneously called bonito.

slack water – top and bottom of the tide when tidal movement stops and the water is 'slack'.

spawning – fish breed by spawning where male fish broadcast milt (sperm) as females release their eggs. Spawning may take place between pairs of fish or in large spawning aggregations of thousands of individuals, depending on the species. Different species spawn at different depths, different water temperatures and at different times of the year. Many species make well-known migrations to spawn in the same area every year.

spinning reel – the most popular style of casting reel with an open face, bail arm and revolving line pickup and winding mechanism. Also called open-face, threadline or eggbeater reels.

strayline(ing) – fishing with minimal weight in relatively shallow water, usually in conjunction with a berley trail, using a strayline rig: hook(s), small sinker or no sinker, slid down the trace onto the hook, trace and swivel or knotted to the mainline.

suicide hooks – a popular hook pattern variously called octopus or beak by different makes.

superbraid – thin, non-stretch lines made from woven or fused, gel-spun polyethylene fibres. Superbraid is incredibly strong for its diameter and its non-stretch properties make it popular with deepwater anglers and those fishers needing to turn fish instantly to avoid snagging up.

surfcaster – someone who surf casts. Also the rod and reel combination used for casting baits and lures into the surf.

swell – waves caused by weather patterns well out to sea. Swells are usually higher than waves with their crests much further apart. It is common to have swell from one direction and wind waves laid over the top of them from quite another direction a messy sea state.

terminal tackle – the stuff at the end of a fishing line: hooks, sinkers, swivels, lures, etc.

terns – small, white, diving seabirds that feed on small fish. Diving terns are a sure sign of pelagic predators feeding below, usually kahawai and jack mackerel but sometimes skipjack tuna, slimy mackerel and others.

tides – the sea is affected by the moon and sun's gravitational forces which draw the ocean's water upwards, causing high tides in one place and low tides elsewhere. In New Zealand and most other places there are four tides in a 24-hour period: two high tides and two low tides.

Tides are much effected by topography, particularly island archipelagos, restricted waterways, large harbours and narrow passages. Tide heights vary from place to place and throughout the month. In some places there are six or more tides per day, while others experience just one high tide and one low tide. Some parts of the world, mostly close to the equator, experience minimal tides.

tidal stream – a current caused by the tide. It can run in any direction and usually, but not always, reverses with the change of the tide.

tinnies – a colloquial term for small aluminium boats, usually dinghies.

tope – school sharks. Small to medium sharks weighing up to 60 kg commonly caught in harbours, off beaches and around reefs in deeper water. Also known as 'lemonfish' or 'fish and chips sharks', they're a good food fish.

trace – part of a rig to which the hook(s) are attached. Traces are usually made up of a length of thicker nylon, fluorocarbon or wire.

trolling – towing a lure/lures behind the boat. Trolling should not be confused with trawling, which is dragging a net behind a boat.

work-up – a feeding frenzy of predatory fish and, usually, birds. Predators push baitfish to the surface where they're accessible to the birds, which often mark the work-up for anglers. Dolphins may or may not be present, also.

Index